Principals in the public

Engaging Community Support

Practical Resources for

Public Engagement, Public Relations, and Marketing

A joint publication of NAESP & NSPRA

ISBN 0-939327-13-9

NAESP
1615 Duke Street
Alexandria, VA 22314-3483
703 / 684-3345
www.naesp.org

NSPRA
15948 Derwood Road
Rockville, MD 20855
301 / 519-0496
www.nspra.org

Acknowledgments

Just as reaching out to communities is not something that can be done by one person, planning a resource guide such as this one is not something that can be accomplished by one organization.

The National Association of Elementary School Principals (NAESP) gratefully acknowledges the support and assistance that were given generously and enthusiastically by both organizations and individuals. They were willing to take time from demanding schedules and responsibilities to share their thoughts, experiences, and expertise in an effort to make *Principals in the Public* a vital component of NAESP's national public engagement campaign, *Our Children — Our Schools — Our Future.*

The National School Public Relations Association (NSPRA) has guided all stages of the development and production of the guide. Led by principal author, Rich Bagin, APR, NSPRA Executive Director, their writers and editors have transformed planning discussions into an organized collection of practical strategies and activities for engaging community support and making effective use of all media in sharing the good news about schools.

Contributing partners — Educational Research Service, Corwin Press, the Center for Developmental Studies, and the Center for Substance Abuse Prevention — have all provided assistance. Cable in the Classroom has added media-related resources for local schools.

Sincere thanks go to the many principals, state association leaders, school district public relations directors, and individuals from across the country who met in focus groups that both informed our work and kept our vision aligned with the reality of life in the schools and communities for which this guide is created.

Our corporate partner, MetLife Resources, has generously made development, production, and dissemination of *Principals in the Public* possible. We deeply appreciate their commitment to this project.

Principals in the Public

Principals in the Public

Dear Colleague:

At no time in the history of our nation's education has the public's perception of schools been so critically important. What parents and the broader community believe to be true about how well we do our job is strongly influenced by the media, and the media isn't always in tune with the positive things that happen every day in good schools. It becomes, then, the responsibility of the principal to get the right messages out to the public and to engage the public in the life of the school in such meaningful ways that reality and perception become one and the same.

The National Association of Elementary School Principals is committed to supporting elementary and middle school leaders in meeting this challenge. *Our Children — Our Schools — Our Future*, chosen as the theme of NAESP's national campaign on engaging community support, underscores the importance of this undertaking. We know that such support cannot be achieved in a short period of time; it is gained only through consistent and ongoing effort.

Principals in the Public is designed for that consistent commitment to the goals of the campaign. Developed in collaboration with the National School Public Relations Association, the guide contains a wealth of strategies and activities that can be implemented in schools from urban to suburban to rural to small communities. There are ideas on how to bring positive media focus to your programs and projects, ways to involve families who are unable to volunteer in traditional ways, pointers on communication with all the various audiences who make up the school community, and basic public relations techniques that work. All can be used successfully in schools to establish and maintain public engagement as a high priority.

NAESP deeply appreciates the generosity of our corporate partner MetLife Resources in making the production of this guide possible and sharing with us a strong commitment to building strong community support for the schools that do, indeed, shape our nation's future.

Sincere good wishes,

Vincent L. Ferrandino

Vincent L. Ferrandino
Executive Director

Principals in the Public

Contents

Packaged separately…

Principals in the Public: Camera-ready Worksheets and Handouts

Principals in the Public

Getting Started

Principals in the Public *is designed for today's busy principal*

The recent National Association of Elementary School Principals (NAESP) 10-year study on the principalship clearly pointed out that communication, marketing, public affairs and public relations, and engagement activities are now given more time and importance than ever before. It used to be that the central office took care of these functions, but today's savvy principals know that they are the key leaders in building support and creating a positive reputation for their schools.

Today's Changing Culture Relates to Public Support

It used to be that our schools could garner all the support they seemed to need just by doing a good job. But as the NAESP study pointed out, times are now different.

Here are some reasons "things have changed" in as little time as the past five years:

❖ *Parents and others seem to want "instant answers" to their inquiries.*
   They are used to quick response times with technology; they think that

---

schools should be as responsive as other organizations that they have become accustomed to.

❖ ***Competition is becoming more prevalent*** — whether it be from for-profit initiatives, new choice programs, an increase in private education, magnet programs, voucher plans, or home schooling.

❖ ***Many parents seem more prone to "shop" for their children's schools*** and are looking for key indicators that their "school of choice" is a good fit for their children. Real estate agents also feed this frenzy.

❖ ***New accountability measures are springing forth at an accelerated rate.*** Schools now have individual report cards by the state, the district, the media, and a battery of additional testing agencies and consumer groups. *Where does your school rank?* is now a question that today's principals often hear.

❖ ***Nearly 80% of the population does not have children in schools in many communities***; this factor breaks down the natural connection to schools and the natural accompanying support of schools.

❖ ***The diversity of our student and family populations is increasing*** and new techniques and efforts are needed to communicate and relate with the changing population.

❖ ***Saving and making the most of time are key priorities for many busy parents and community leaders***. Like principals, most parents and others view themselves as being extremely busy and not having time to attend school meetings or become involved in their schools.

Community support may seem to be waning. Some barometers, such as the annual Gallup Poll and recent studies by the Public Agenda Foundation, indicate that the public is becoming more skeptical about public education in general.

But the good news is that the public still rates its local schools about twice as high as other public schools around the nation.

How do people rate their local schools?

In the latest Gallup Poll in 1999, nearly half of those polled (49%) give their local schools an A or B, compared to 24% giving an A or B to public schools around the country.

In the latest Gallup Poll in 1999, nearly half of those polled (49%) give their local schools an A or B, compared to 24% giving an A or B to public schools around the country. So, in one sense, the local elementary and middle schools do have a base of public support to work on. If nearly half of those polled feel that we are doing a good job, we are on our way to building even greater support for our schools.

Public Support Builds a Great School

Why do we need even greater public support? Ask principals who work in schools that have support and they will tell you that in their schools staff morale is high, student achievement is climbing, students want to come to school, real estate agents have their schools on the "A" list, and the central office always makes sure that visiting dignitaries stop at their schools. Parent, business, and community groups are involved in their schools and many of these schools have won the prestigious national blue ribbon award.

How do busy principals chart a path to engage community support for their schools?

Taking a Look at Public Engagement

First we need to look at what we mean by public engagement.

David Mathews, author of *Is There a Public for Public Schools*, noted that the community is the universe and all other entities — such as schools — are satellites revolving around the universe. This community-centered approach then leads to the statement,

> **"Ask not what your community can do for your schools, but rather what your schools can do for your community."**

The Mathews model, however, serves as a wake-up call for all educators when it comes to engaging support for their schools.

The Annenberg Institute recently completed a study on how public engagement works in school communities and found, for the most part, that true public engagement — the bottom-up, community-conversation approach — was not found in a majority of schools and school districts across America.

But in joint workshops, Annenberg and the National School Public Relations Association (NSPRA) did find that in many locations today, parents are less likely to be content with just understanding a school's goals and decisions.

Some parents and others want a different level of "engagement." They want to know how decisions are made. They want a transparent administration of their school so they can see how it works and how to solve a problem — if and when one occurs. They seek more meaningful substance when they donate their precious time to the schools.

Another description of engagement notes that people today want to be served, not sold, and involved, not told.

This "open and transparent leadership role" is causing a shift in the way business and organizations communicate and build relationships. If you ask 10 people to define public engagement, most likely you will receive 10 different and correct answers.

People want to be served, not sold, and involved, not told.

Public engagement in its strictest sense of being a completely transparent process is rare in schools and organizations because it calls for a major commitment of time and relinquishment of authority by principals, teachers, superintendents, and school board members.

But in today's schools where relationship-building is key to future success, numerous forms of public engagement activities are being successfully practiced by schools around the country.

Public engagement as it is now being used by organizations and schools calls for skills in public relations, public affairs, marketing, communication, and organizational management. The process of public engagement places a high priority on listening to key audiences and then jointly rolling up your sleeves and working as partners to do what is best for all children in your school community.

> **P**ublic engagement calls for skills in public relations, public affairs, marketing, communication, and organizational management.

This guide is designed to help busy principals increase community support for their schools. It will take into account all the tools you need to accomplish that goal. This guide is anchored in practical ideas and advice; it is not designed to serve as a research project full of theory and footnotes that will not add to the mission of increasing support for your school. It combines the elements of communication, public relations, marketing, and engagement into one practical guide.

Getting Started

The first step to take is to ask:

❖ What do we mean when we say we want our school to be engaged with the community?

This question is quickly followed by:

❖ What do we want the engagement process to do for our schools?

❖   What do we want the public engagement process to do for our community?

Most busy principals will probably begin by focusing on what engagement can do for their schools. Ask:

❖   What gaps or shortcomings does your school have where support from the community can help you?

❖   How can the public's engagement make your school better?

These questions can be answered by pulling your staff and parent groups together to honestly assess how public engagement can make your school even better than it is today. What could be accomplished with extra support from business, community leaders, parents, and volunteers?

The form on the following page may help you in this process. A reproducible copy of it is also included in the camera-ready section.

(*Note:*   Please read through the remainder of this guide before you implement this component because you will learn of more than 50 additional ways to engage your community to build support in your school.)

Principals in the Public

Setting a Direction for Public Engagement in Your School

1. What is your definition of public engagement? Give a few concrete examples of the definition in action.

2. List the types of publics that you hope to engage in your school.

3. Brainstorm ways that the public can help make your school better.

4. Narrow the list to three or four public engagement activities that may be effective for your school in the next two years.

5. Assign staff or parent leaders to serve on action committees to develop a plan for each of the public engagement activities.

Public Engagement Activity: _____

Chair of task force: _____

Members of task force: _____   _____

_____   _____

_____   _____

_____   _____

_____   _____

Deadline for project description: ____/____/____

1: Getting Started   9   **NAESP / NSPRA**

One of the best ways to start thinking about increasing support for your school is to first learn about the techniques that are most effective in engagement, communication, public relations, and marketing.

> **F**irst learn about the techniques that are most effective in engagement, communication, public relations, and marketing.

Many educators believe that creating a brochure or a new website will be the best ways to communicate and engage their various publics to increase school support; however, research and years of professional practice of communications in schools tell us differently.

Always remember the maxim that,

People beat paper just about every time.

Interpersonal relationship-building techniques are the most effective way of engaging today's parents and others on school issues. It is difficult for parents to ask questions of a brochure.

And even if your website is interactive, it is not nearly as powerful as asking the question directly of you, the principal, or one of your teachers.

Brochures and websites in your plan build support, but don't expect to increase support without the key interpersonal relationship-building techniques found sprinkled throughout this kit.

M. Frederic Volkman of Washington University in St. Louis, has designed the following *Hierarchy of Effective Communication* to drive home this point.

Hierarchy of Effective Communication

- ❖ One-to-one, face-to-face
- ❖ Small group discussion or meeting
- ❖ Speaking before a large group
- ❖ Phone conversation
- ❖ Hand-written, personal note
- ❖ Typewritten, personal letter, not a form letter or email (editor's addition)
- ❖ Personal "form letter"
- ❖ Mass-produced, non-personal letter
- ❖ Brochure or pamphlet sent out as a direct mail piece
- ❖ Articles in organizational newsletter, magazine, tabloid
- ❖ News carried in popular press
- ❖ Advertising in newspapers, radio, television, magazines, posters, etc.
- ❖ Others — billboards, pens, give-aways, etc.

So, as you begin to think about ways to build support, start thinking about the methods that you now use to communicate with all your key audiences — students, staff, parents, community leaders, and neighbors of your school.

Remember that *People beat paper just about every time.*

People beat paper just about every time.

 Getting Started on Building Support

A Principal's Checklist

1. Do you encourage teachers at your school to send notes home commending children for the smallest of accomplishments?

2. Do you frequently remind your staff to take five minutes at the close of the school day to review the major points of instruction covered during the day?

3. Do you encourage teachers at least once a month to channel information through your office which can be the source of a news story for your newsletters, your website, or the media?

4. Do you give disgruntled parents a chance to "sound off," especially if they are angry or upset?

5. Do you send home a note or commendation for a child's noteworthy accomplishments?

6. Do you belong to a community service club or organization?

7. In the last month, has your school been a host for a mini-tour of senior citizens, real estate agents, service club members, parents who are not PTA officers, parochial school representatives, or others?

8. During this school year, have you encouraged your teachers to offer or suggest a program involving their students and themselves for an educational presentation at a service club meeting or another community event?

9. Do you encourage teachers and PTA members to write about proposed legislation or current conditions concerning education?

10. Do you remind your staff often to involve parents and others in classroom activity?

11. Do you occasionally drop in at the home of a child who has been having unusual difficulty of some kind?

12. Do you encourage your staff to use community resource people for visits and talks in the classroom?

13. Do you invite elementary parents to take turns (by classrooms) having lunch with their children?

14. Does your school have a "buddy" system or big sisters or brothers to help newcomers (both staff and students) feel more at ease in their new school surroundings?

15. Have you made arrangements to schedule coffee hours at least once a month in the home of someone in the community *during the evening* for parents who work to meet with you?

16. Have you made arrangements to schedule coffee hours at least once a month at the school *during the day* so you can meet with small groups of parents (those who are not PTA officers)?

17. Do you have a bulletin board in a central hallway where articles concerning your school, staff, and pupils can be displayed? (Upper grade students can handle this assignment.)

18. Do you encourage PTA officers to schedule short educational presentations by small groups of students with their teachers at PTA meetings?

19. Do you have a "Hall of Fame" bulletin board where photographs, brief biographies, or newspaper accounts about former students can be displayed?

20. Do you insist that your office staff follow telephone techniques in a friendly, courteous, and understandable manner?

21. Have you noticed whether visitors to the office (either parents or students) are acknowledged promptly and helped in a friendly, understandable manner?

22. Are your outer office and your personal office neat and uncluttered?

23. Have you taken any postgraduate courses recently in public relations, communication, or school-community relations?

24. Do you write notes to teachers to commend them for unusual, successful, or outstanding accomplishments?

25. Do you have a full staff meeting at least once a year involving custodians, office personnel, food service employees, and teachers so they may all have an opportunity to meet and discuss common problems?

26. Do you always communicate with your staff, students, and parents well before any major change or implementation of new decisions?

27. Do you encourage teachers to participate in community activities?

28. Have you begun using technology — e-mail, voice-mail — to assist with your communication efforts?

29. Have you and your staff communicated what your school stands for and developed key messages to be repeated throughout the year?

30. Do you train and coach staff for parent conferences and Back-to-School night?

31. Do you make an effort to reach out to non-English speaking parents?

32. Do you know the name, address, and contact numbers for the local media?

33. Do you have a crisis communication plan?

34. Is your school seen as a "Good Neighbor" in the local community?

35. Do you periodically seek community "influentials" to participate in a Principal for a Day Program?

36. Do you encourage volunteers to assist in your school? Do you have volunteers other than parents of your current students?

37. Do you use your outdoor message boards for substantive achievement messages?

38. Do you use the four-point communication test when decisions are made:

    — Who needs to know this?

    — What do they need to know?

    — What is the best time and vehicle to communicate this?

    — And how will we know the message has been received?

39. Does every newsletter give your parents and others something to brag about?

40. Do you publicly praise all staff and students for their accomplishments?

2 Research

Research — A Critical Component to Communication

One of the more costly mistakes you can make is not completing some research to guide your communication effort. The mistake is costly because you may be spending time and money on communication techniques that are not effective for your particular audiences.

It is always better to know what your audiences know and feel about your school before you embark on your communication effort. You don't necessarily have to complete formal research that may be too time-consuming and expensive, but you will need to know what your key target audiences already know, think, and feel about your school.

You can use the information you collect to determine what messages are needed and what the best ways are of getting those messages to your key audiences.

First, Learn from the Research of Others

Both NAESP and NSPRA have collected research on topics that involve dealing with parents — where parents get most of their information and just how involved parents may want to be in your school.

Where do parents receive their information?

According to NSPRA surveys over the years, we found that most parents receive their information about your school from:

❖ their children,

❖ the neighborhood children,

❖ teachers, and

❖ other parents — in that order.

The school secretary also ranks in the top five suppliers of information — followed by *you*, the school principal. School and classroom newsletters, PTA meetings, lunch menus, and websites round out the top 10.

Time after time, with little fluctuation, these results are confirmed when working with schools throughout the United States and Canada. Notice that people don't see the local media as a major source of information about their local school. So, when you think about your school's communication efforts in reaching parents, make sure that you keep your students and staff informed because they are your key communicators about your school.

NAESP also recommends that principals be prepared to answer *The 10 Most Important Questions About Their School*.

The 10 Most Important Questions About a School

1. What is the classroom-to-student ratio?

2. Does the school have a well-equipped and well-used library or media center?

3. Does the reading program balance whole language and phonics?

4. How are computers used for instruction?

5. What is the school's disciplinary policy?

6. What is the teaching philosophy? (Lecturing, group, individual, team?)

7. Do professional specialists support the school program?

8. How is student progress reported? (Grading practices, portfolios)

9. How often are textbooks and classroom materials reviewed and updated?

10. Can parents meet with teachers other than during traditional school hours?

NAESP also recommends that principals become aware of the five most critical things that parents should observe in a school.

The Five Most Critical Things Parents Should Observe in a School

1. Do students appear actively involved in learning?

2. Do teachers appear to manage classroom discipline effectively?

3. Is students' work prominently displayed in classrooms and hallways?

4. Are parents and others warmly welcomed as visitors?

5. Is the school clean and in good repair inside and out?

The Public Agenda Foundation, based in New York City, has completed numerous studies that are pertinent to building your school's engagement and communication efforts. The good news is that, according to the foundation's findings, *most parents and community leaders are supportive of our schools and the challenge to keep improving our schools.*

Most parents believe that all children need to be grounded in the basics (reading and writing, mathematics and science, and basic use of computers) before students are given additional academic challenges. People generally believe that schools have to be safe havens for all children. And most parents agree that if they had more time to spend at their child's school, they would prefer to spend it helping their child improve. (You can find more information about all the Public Agenda studies on the foundation's website at www.publicagenda.org.)

Combined, this information from NAESP, NSPRA, and the Public Agenda Foundation, gives you ideas about the messages you may wish to communicate and some of the key communicators of that information.

Then Complete Your Own Research

But the best way to learn about building support for your school with your key audiences, is to complete your own research. How do you find out why your key audiences know about your school? As simple as it sounds, you ask, and then you listen.

Ways to Listen...

Focus groups are a great way to capture some honest feedback about your school. Schools often use consultants to facilitate the process, but we urge you to oversee it yourself.

Having a neutral face is important, but that face could be another member of your school district's administration or even a member of the community. In all cases, make sure that the facilitator knows what he or she is expected to do and train the facilitator so that both of you feel comfortable with the process.

What to do?

❖ **Invite your selected target audience** (such as current, prospective, or outgoing parents; staff; students; community leaders; real estate representatives, etc.) by letter. Then follow up with a phone call.

❖ **Call the participants the day before** the scheduled session to remind them that you value their input.

❖ ***Conduct two or three focus groups on the same topic or issue.*** Once you begin hearing the same responses from a set of questions, you will start to see a pattern and build a baseline of what people know, think, and feel about your school.

Some other ground rules include:

❖ ***Be sure that the group is not too big*** — preferably fewer than 10 people.

❖ ***Don't make the group too homogeneous*** — watch for fair representation of your school community.

❖ ***Set clear ground rules*** that establish value to all remarks by participants. There are no right or wrong answers and there's no need to argue a point. (A good facilitator will know just when to leave a point or ask a few more questions about a topic.)

❖ ***Meet in a comfortable room***; have refreshments available.

❖ ***Stick to your announced timetable***.

❖ ***Keep the session confidential***. Make sure that everyone knows that their names will not be placed with their comments. Anonymity breeds frank answers.

Sample questions for focus groups

Here are some focus group questions related to communication that you may want to consider using:

1. What does this school stand for?

2. What would you like it to stand for?

3. What's right about this school?

4. What needs improving?

5. What would you need to see to believe that this school is improving?

6. How do you receive information about this school?

7. What is your preferred way of receiving information about the school? How often do you want to receive this information?

8. I have here some communication vehicles now used by the school (the PTA newsletter, school newsletter, brochures, school paper, classroom newsletters, a print-out of pages from the website, email, voicemail, etc.): What is your opinion of these techniques? What should we doing more of? What doesn't work for you?

9. Would you say that this school is approachable? Or would you say it has a distant, somewhat bureaucratic personality?

10. Do you use the Internet from home or work to communicate? How? Should our school do more of this? If yes, what types of topics would you like to see covered?

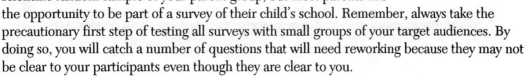

Surveys are another way of listening to your target audiences. Once again, you can spend a great deal of time and money on surveys, but our advice for these efforts is to keep them extremely practical and simple.

Often surveys are completed with the assistance of volunteer parents and the survey instruments are also given to all parents. (Make sure you have translations completed for those schools with a high population of non-English speaking parents.) If you prefer, you can complete a scientific random sample of your parent group, but most parents like the opportunity to be part of a survey of their child's school. Remember, always take the precautionary first step of testing all surveys with small groups of your target audiences. By doing so, you will catch a number of questions that will need reworking because they may not be clear to your participants even though they are clear to you.

Communication survey

The following survey on communications has been used by principals around the country.

❖ *Parent Involvement Can Be Fun*

Parent Survey

Your local school believes that good communication with parents is in the best interest of the child and in the development of the school program to meet his or her individual needs.

With this in mind, would you take a few minutes to answer the following questions? Since you don't have to sign the questionnaire, please respond as frankly as you can.

1. Check the sources from which you receive most of your information about your child's school:

❑ Newspaper
   ❑ Daily
   ❑ Weekly
❑ Radio
❑ Television
❑ Principal
❑ Teachers
❑ School meetings

❑ Other parents
❑ Your child
❑ Printed materials from the school
❑ The central office of the school system
❑ Other (Please specify.)

_____

_____

2. Overall, which of the following statements best describes your child's school?
   - ❏ Keeps us fully informed
   - ❏ Gives us some information
   - ❏ Gives us little information
   - ❏ Gives no information

3. When your child's school gives you information about its programs, which one of the following statements reflects your feelings?
   - ❏ Always complete and accurate
   - ❏ Usually complete and accurate
   - ❏ Seldom complete and accurate
   - ❏ Never complete and accurate

4. When you have a question or problem about school, who do you usually contact first?
   - ❏ The principal
   - ❏ A classroom teacher
   - ❏ A school secretary
   - ❏ The child's counselor
   - ❏ Someone in the system's central office
   - ❏ Another parent
   - ❏ Someone on the Board of Education
   - ❏ Other (Please explain.) _____

5. Do you usually get action from the person you checked above?
   - ❏ Yes
   - ❏ No

6. When the school has a PTA meeting or special program, what is your usual reaction?
   - ❏ I try to go because I know it is important.
   - ❏ I try to go when I think the topic is useful.
   - ❏ I try to go, but it's usually not worth the time.
   - ❏ I should go more often, but I don't seem to find the time.
   - ❏ I usually never attend school meetings for various reasons.

7. How often do you attend parent-teacher conferences?
    - ❏   Every time they are scheduled.
    - ❏   Only when I think my child is having a problem.
    - ❏   I have never attended such a conference.

8. Which of the following groups are available to parents at your school? Please check all that apply:
    - ❏   PTA
    - ❏   Advisory boards
    - ❏   Room mother's group
    - ❏   Mothers' club
    - ❏   Fathers' club
    - ❏   Volunteer programs

9. Each school tries to communicate with its local community on the topics listed below. Check the amount of information that you feel you have received from your local school on the following topics.

Topic	About the right amount of information	Not enough information	Never received any information
The school's program in…			
— math	❏	❏	❏
— science	❏	❏	❏
— reading/language arts	❏	❏	❏
— creative arts	❏	❏	❏
— social studies	❏	❏	❏
The school's policies and rules	❏	❏	❏
School system rules and policies	❏	❏	❏
The progress and achievement of my child	❏	❏	❏
Quality and achievement of school's staff	❏	❏	❏
New methods and materials used in school	❏	❏	❏

10. For each topic listed below, check the source of your information. If you receive information about the topics from more than one source, please check all that apply.

	Teachers	Building principal	Your child	Other parents	Board of Education	PTA meetings	Parent-teacher conferences	School meetings	Parent handbook	Newspaper	Radio	Broadcast TV	Cable TV	My school newspaper or newsletter	Home-page
Local school policies and rules															
School system's policies and rules															
Progress and achievement of my child															
Quality and achievement of school staff															
New methods and materials used in the school program															
School curriculum or subject areas															
The reputation of my child's school															

Climate surveys

Principals are often asked to assess the school climate in their building by asking questions of parents, staff members, and students. Since each school is different, the editors of this tool kit felt it would be more practical to give you a "Question Bank" of possible questions to include in your school's climate survey.

These are the most-often asked questions in school climate surveys. Choose those that seem appropriate for you. Most of the questions can be answered on a point scale:

❖ Strongly Agree,

❖ Agree,

❖ Uncertain,

❖ Disagree, or

❖ Strongly Disagree.

School climate question bank:

Parents

1. Our school has a plan to promote school/community interaction.

2. Our school has regular joint school/community activities.

3. Our parents feel welcome in our school.

4. Our parents work cooperatively with teachers to improve student progress.

5. Our district/school parent education program meets the needs of our school community.

6. Our school faculty and staff are committed to the goals of the school.

7. Our students show mutual respect for one another.

8. Our school personnel show mutual respect for one another.

9. Procedures for resolving conflict are applied fairly and consistently in our school by the appropriate staff according to the situation.

10. The school and school grounds are clean, aesthetically pleasing, safe, and well-maintained.

11. Our students are enthusiastic about learning.

12. Our teachers are enthusiastic about teaching.

13. Our parents demonstrate interest in and concern for their children's school.

14. Our student morale is high.

15. Our staff morale is high.

16. Our community morale is high.

17. Students support one another and work together harmoniously.

18. School personnel support one another and work together harmoniously.

19. School pride is evident among students.

20. School pride is evident among staff.

21. School pride is evident among the community.

22. The teachers know and address students by name.

23. The principal knows and addresses students by name.

24. Our school personnel serve as models and reward appropriate behavior.

25. Our school has a written code of conduct.

26. Our code of conduct is developed cooperatively by students, staff, and parents.

27. Our school code is followed consistently.

28. Our students, staff, and parents accept and share responsibility for discipline.

29. Discipline is used as a tool for learning rather than as a punishment.

30. The accomplishments of students are appropriately recognized.

31. The accomplishments of school personnel are appropriately recognized.

32. Student work in our school is attractively displayed.

33. Our students are aware that outstanding performance is expected of them.

34. Our staff is aware that outstanding performance is expected of them.

35. Our students expect to be successful.

36. Our staff expects to be successful.

37. School personnel believe that all children can learn.

38. I feel welcome at my child's school.

39. This school is preparing my child for the future.

40. The staff has my child's best interests at heart.

41. The school staff treats my child with respect.

42. This school provides a positive learning environment.

43. The staff listens to the issues or concerns I raise.

44. The school encourages my child to learn.

Staff

1. This school building is a pleasant place to work.

2. Teachers think that parents should stay away from school unless they are called in for a specific reason.

3. The principal tries to improve the teachers' working conditions.

4. Students are disruptive in class.

5. The principal sets an example by working beyond the normal school day.

6. Teachers think of parents as partners in educating children.

7. The principal is accessible to teachers.

8. Students stay on-task during classroom activities.

9. Toilet facilities are usually in poor condition.

10. Teachers' closest friends are other faculty from this school.

11. Teachers are interested in what students do outside of school.

12. Parents and teachers try to communicate with each other.

13. Students are enthusiastically involved with classroom activities.

14. Teachers have a comfortable place where they can gather.

15. Students ask teachers questions when they do not understand.

16. Teachers are friendly with students.

17. Teachers socialize together during the school day.

18. There is conflict between parents and teachers.

19. The principal tries to motivate teachers to work to their full capacity.

20. Teachers invite other faculty members to their homes.

21. Teachers go out of their way to understand students.

22. Students actively participate in discussions.

23. The faculty is proud when visitors see the school building.

24. Faculty meetings are well organized.

25. Teachers at this school keep to themselves.

26. Students do not respect their teachers.

27. This school should be cleaner than it usually is.

28. Parents are involved in this school's activities.

29. Teachers and students can solve their disagreements.

30. Teachers encourage parental involvement in school.

31. Parents are encouraged to participate in school-sponsored activities.

32. Teachers take a personal interest in students.

33. Students are bored in school.

34. The school grounds are often littered.

35. Students often fight with one another.

36. Teachers are not interested in talking with parents about their children.

37. Students like their teachers.

38. Teachers encourage students to work hard.

39. The school building is clean.

40. Students respect one another.

41. Parents feel uncomfortable about going to see a teacher.

42. Teachers make students feel important.

43. Teachers explain schoolwork clearly.

44. School property is often damaged.

45. Students help one another.

46. Parents are well informed about what is going on in school.

47. Teachers often say nice things about students.

48. Students work hard in school.

49. The school building is a comfortable place for students.

50. Students are friendly.

51. The school building looks nice.

52. It is hard for students to make friends.

Students

1. I feel welcome at this school.

2. Teachers in this school care about me.

3. My teachers help me to be eager and excited about learning.

4. I am given challenging work at this school.

5. I do challenging work in the computer lab.

6. I receive assistance in the library to help me learn more about my school subjects.

7. I am learning a lot at this school.

8. This school does a good job of letting me know about school rules.

9. I think that my school work is graded fairly.

10. The principal in this school is interested in the students.

11. My teachers will provide extra help if I need it.

12. My homework helps me do better in school.

13. I usually understand how to do my homework.

14. Students in my classroom are well behaved.

15. I am learning about the dangers of alcohol, tobacco, and drugs.

16. I feel safe when I go to and from school.

17. I feel safe when I am at school.

18. This school has a good playground.

19. I enjoy school most of the time.

20. I am proud of my school.

21. Students in this school show a lot of school spirit.

22. Much of my school work is boring.

23. Much of my school work is interesting and useful.

24. The office staff is helpful to the students.

25. The health office staff is helpful to the students.

26. When I have a concern, my teacher will listen to me.

27. This school has a good variety of after school activities.

28. This school's discipline policies are enforced fairly.

29. This school encourages me to do my best.

30. Most students are involved in special school events and school activities.

31. Using the computer is a good way for me to learn my school subjects.

32. There are so many students in my classroom that my teacher doesn't always have time to help me if I need it.

33. Students should dress more appropriately for school.

34. Students from different backgrounds and cultures work and play together in the same school activities.

35. Students are often given grades to show the quality of their work. Suppose your school was graded the same way. What grade would you give your school?

Additional Research Steps to Take to Make Your Schools' Program More Effective

It's often valuable to step back and look at the opportunities you have each year to enhance your relationship with targeted audiences. A staff meeting exercise is to review the following critical communication opportunities during your regular school year.

These opportunities are not always thought of as a time to communicate about your school, but most parents and others use these events to begin building or reinforcing the opinion they have of your school. For most schools, these opportunities include:

- ❖ PTA/Home school meetings

- ❖ Registration packet/meeting

- ❖ Visits before school begins/orientations

- ❖ Open House or Back-to-School Nights

- ❖ Parent-Teacher conferences

- ❖ Report cards

- ❖ Picnics

- ❖ Field trips

- ❖ Fund-raising events

- ❖ Field days

- ❖ First Friday events

- ❖ Newsletters

- ❖ Web site

❖ Faxes

❖ Written/Verbal correspondence with principals/teachers including email
   and voicemail

❖ Add your own:

❖ Add your own:

All of the above opportunities are reputation-builders or breakers. They are the ongoing
activities that can enhance your communication program when your staff realizes they are
wonderful opportunities to help build continued support for your school.

Community Outlets for School Information

Often, school leaders overlook obvious community outlets where
they can place their yearbooks, school newspapers, school
newsletters, and updates of accomplishments.

❖ First, **look at your immediate attendance areas** for community spots,
   such as municipal buildings, waiting rooms of doctors' offices, quick-lube
   auto shops, libraries, and senior citizen centers.

❖ Also, make sure that **copies are sent out and displayed in your feeder
   schools and nursery schools** in your system.

❖ Next, **find out where many of your parents work**; see if extra copies can
   be sent to their workplaces.

As more and more outlets are used, your entire community will learn a great deal more about your school. (*In the camera-ready section of this package, you'll find a reproducible copy of the following worksheet.*)

Outlets in our attendance area

_____   _____

_____   _____

_____   _____

Feeder schools and nursery schools

_____   _____

_____   _____

_____   _____

Parent workplaces

_____   _____

_____   _____

_____   _____

_____   _____

_____   _____

And Finally, Five More Ways to Listen...

❶ Question/Idea Cards

You can place 4″x 6″Question/Idea cards or half sheets of paper in "public spots" in your building — especially during major events when more parents and other residents may be visiting your building. Make sure you respond to the question and ideas within a week after you receive them.

❷ Email/Voicemail/Website Communication

Make sure your audiences know that these systems can be two-way. Refer to the technology section in this guide for more details on how to use these devices for feedback.

❸ Breakfast Communication Clubs

Once a month invite a mix of parents, community leaders, and staff to a breakfast meeting with you. Have just a few agenda items handy — perhaps 10 minutes' worth, and then fill the remaining 35 minutes or so by listening. Send a thank you note to those who participated. You may want to ask your PTA and school site council president to "listen" along with you at these breakfast meetings.

❹ Questions/Answers in Newsletters

You may want to start a question-and-answer section in your newsletter. Ask parents to submit questions. You can answer them directly and then include the most relevant in your newsletter.

❺ Secretary's/Counselor's Scanning

At least once every two weeks, check with your school secretary or guidance counselor about the types of repeated calls they receive from parents. Include information about those calls in your daily bulletin, newsletter, and website.

Principals in the Public

3 *Planning*

Create a Communication Plan and Implement It

Attempting to communicate without first having a plan is like starting your vacation without knowing where you are going. Yet, far too frequently, educators begin communicating without deciding who the key audiences are, how those audiences will receive the information, what the communication objective is, or even where and how to find the resources for the project.

Annual Communication Plan

Every school draws up an annual calendar of events showing holidays, Back-to-School events, report card dates, parent conferences, etc. Most of these events have a communication component — notices to be taken home to parents, an ad or story to be run in the community newspaper, information to be prepared in advance.

Once your annual calendar of events is drawn up, you need to create a communication plan to implement it. The communication planning for parent conferences, for example, would indicate:

❖ **Who do we need to inform?** — parents, teachers, and other school staff

❖ **When will they need the information?** — several weeks before conference times

❖ **What types of information will they need?** — dates, times, location, how to make appointments, hints on preparing for the conferences for both teachers and parents

❖ **Who's responsible for which tasks?** —preparing and mailing notices, obtaining materials for teachers and parents on how to make conferences successful

❖ **Where will any funds come from?**

Annual Projects or Goals

As part of accountability efforts or meeting school/district objectives, most schools focus on several goals each year to improve student learning. Most of these goals involve efforts to be undertaken throughout the school year, leading to a change in behaviors.

How you plan for and communicate about these projects or goals may be a significant factor in the success of your efforts.

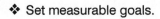
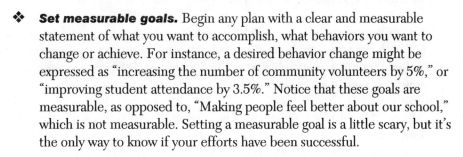

How do you create your plan?

- ❖ Set measurable goals.
- ❖ Determine deadlines and resources.
- ❖ Involve your staff in planning.
- ❖ Determine your priority publics.
- ❖ Find out what your audiences know or believe.
- ❖ Develop the plan.
- ❖ Communicate the plan.

❖ **Set measurable goals.** Begin any plan with a clear and measurable statement of what you want to accomplish, what behaviors you want to change or achieve. For instance, a desired behavior change might be expressed as "increasing the number of community volunteers by 5%," or "improving student attendance by 3.5%." Notice that these goals are measurable, as opposed to, "Making people feel better about our school," which is not measurable. Setting a measurable goal is a little scary, but it's the only way to know if your efforts have been successful.

❖ **Determine deadlines and resources.** Once the goal is clearly spelled out, you should set a deadline by which the desired behavior will be achieved and estimate the resources that will you'll need to accomplish it.

❖ ***Involve your staff in planning.*** As you know, you build commitment to goals and plans through the broad involvement of "stakeholders." Stakeholders will have ideas that help make the plan better, and you need their help and commitment.

At the end of this chapter are several worksheets you can use to involve stakeholders at meetings.

— The first can be used to identify the "publics" with whom you need to communicate.

— The second will show the extent to which you are currently communicating with each public.

— The third outlines a format for a School Communication Plan.

❖ ***Determine your priority publics.*** With the goal, deadline, and resources established, one of the most important planning steps is to determine the key audiences with whom you need to communicate, what knowledge and perceptions each has about the issue, and the best way to communicate with them. This process is called "targeting" audiences.

All too frequently, educators send one message to everyone in the same manner and with the same emphasis. That technique might work if there was only one big audience concerned with education, but there are clearly many different constituencies or audiences.

Schools deal with two general audience categories — internal and external. Internal audiences are those within the school family (teachers, classified employees, students, administrators, central office personnel, etc.) External audiences may include the news media, real estate agents, senior citizens, business leaders, prospective students, etc.

Schools deal with two general audience categories — Internal and external.

It's impossible to send the same message to each audience and meet all those audiences' needs.

Some audiences, such as parents and school vendors, may be hard to place, but the point is that a school communicates with all these groups.

Each has different information needs and each places various degrees of credibility on different information sources. Through brainstorming, your staff could identify 50 or more audiences in both broad groups.

It's impossible to send the same message to each audience and meet all those audiences' needs. You must determine which audiences need to hear the messages you will send. For example, if your school is adopting a new discipline policy, your priority is to communicate that information to students, teachers, parents, and other school staff. It is not as urgent for vendors and senior citizens to hear about this.

You must also consider the delivery system for messages to specific audiences. For example, a school newsletter may effectively communicate with parents, but it's unlikely to reach senior citizens.

❖ ***Find out what your audiences know or believe.*** After targeting the audiences for your project and determining the channels of communication that will reach them effectively, it's important to know what knowledge and perceptions each of the audiences has. That might involve using a questionnaire or survey.

An inexpensive way of getting people's opinions is through focus groups.

Another part of research may be examining data to pinpoint particular problem areas. For instance, focusing on a relatively small group of students and their parents, as opposed to all students and parents, may be the key to improving student attendance. School attendance records will quickly indicate which students have the poorest attendance records.

The role of this research in the planning process is to identify:

— Who your key audiences are,

— How best to communicate with each of them, and

— What their knowledge and perceptions are.

❖ **Develop the plan.** Once you decide on the result you want to achieve, know which audiences you need to target, and what they think about the issue, you must plan a strategy to get from the present condition to the result you want.

In this part of the process, you must deal with issues such as:

— **What messages do you need to send to each audience?** That will be based on what you found out about their interests, concerns, and perceptions.

— **What channels of communication will be most effective to reach each audience?** How much can you do through mass communication? How much can you accomplish through interpersonal means?

— **Who will be responsible for each facet of the plan, and what are the deadlines?**

— **How will you know if you were successful?** What evaluation measures will you use to see if you reached your goals?

Target Audiences for Key Issues

This outline may help you pinpoint key audiences as they relate to specific issues for your school. Use a separate page for each target audience: (*See the tool kit for a reproducible copy.*)

1. Issue   _____

2. Audience   _____

3. What do we want this audience to do for us on this issue?

              _____

4. What does this audience know of this issue now?

              _____

5. Assumed best ways to reach this audience _____

6. Who influences this audience on this issue?

              _____

7. Message that will work for this audience on this issue

              _____

              _____

8. Major barriers to accomplishing our goal with this audience

              _____

9. Ways of overcoming those barriers   _____

❖ ***Communicate the plan.*** A plan will be useful only if everyone involved understands the objective, knows what is to happen and when, and realizes how each element fits into the total strategy.

To ensure that this occurs, a plan must be written and distributed to each person responsible for each step.

If a plan requires multiple strategies, develop a series of steps to achieve each one. Each step should describe:

— the planned activity

— the budget (if any)

— beginning and completion dates

— the people responsible for the activity.

A Targeted School Communication Plan

Here's a excerpt of a building level plan for a middle school.

Goal: To increase the number of 5th and 4th grade parents who believe that the middle school climate is a positive one for students.

Primary Audiences: 5th and 4th grade parents.

— *Key Influences on Primary Audiences* — Students, other parents, elementary school and middle school teachers, admissions directors of private schools, parent leaders, and students.

Objectives:

1. Increase direct contacts that 4th and 5th grade parents have with elementary school and middle school teachers.

2. Increase the number of community members who have first-hand experiences in the middle school.

3. Increase the information flow about the middle school concept to both primary audiences and key influentials.

Research/Analysis: Supporters of the middle school program have voiced worries about negative rumors, negative press, and parents who transfer their children to other schools.

Take corrective action, and send more positive messages to make 4th and 5th graders and their parents more comfortable with the transition to the middle high school.

Additional Research Needed:

■ Examine available research on the middle school concept from the National Middle School Association and the National Association of Elementary School Principals (NAESP.)

- Conduct focus groups of 4th and 5th grade parents to pinpoint their perceived concerns and ways to overcome them.
- Confirm or refute perceptions by analyzing the middle school program.

Action:

Steps for Objective 1

1. Host the traditional 5th grade parent meeting in the new presentation room. Invite 4th grade parents to attend as well. Develop a PowerPoint presentation focusing on the concerns mentioned in the focus groups. Offer building tours conducted by 8th grade students.

2. Invite 8th grade parents for coffee with incoming 6th grade parents throughout the year. Give the 5th grade parents a chance to meet the principal and give them a chance to sit in on a class if they wish.

Steps for Objective 2

1. Offer to hold feeder school parent meetings in the middle school.

2. Begin offering free tickets to special events at the middle school to senior citizens, staff of feeder schools, and community leaders.

3. Invite the Rotary Club to have an annual luncheon meeting at the middle school. Conduct student-led tours of the building.

Steps for Objective 3

1. Encourage teachers to contact the communication office about instructional activities in their classrooms.

2. Increase the frequency of *Principally Speaking* from five issues a year to eight.

3. Recruit students (perhaps those on the Principal's List) to write tips for incoming 6th graders about school events, dances,

participation in activities and other topics of interest and concern. Distribute during the summer or during orientation.

4. Review current communications with parents of 5th graders to see if they are user-friendly and up to date.

5. Invite the parent organizations of other schools in the district to appoint a representative to attend the middle school parents group meetings.

Evaluation:

1. Survey parents of 6th graders in November. Ask how well their children made the transition and seek feedback for improvement.

2. Track open enrollment withdrawals between 5th and 6th grade. A diminishing number over the next 2-5 years will indicate success.

3. Conduct an attitude survey among elementary and middle school parents in two years. Compare results with previous surveys.

Planning document

To help you develop a plan for your school, on the next page is a planning document. You'll find a reproducible copy of it in the camera-ready section. Duplicate it for use by your planning team.

Communication/Engagement Planner
for School Buildings

Step 1: *Important consideration*

Make sure your communication effort enhances the mission of your school and fits into the strategic plan of your school and school district. It will then boost the internal positive reputation you are building through this effort.

Step 2: *Target audiences*

List your priority publics, both internal and external.

Internal

_____

_____

_____

_____

External

_____

_____

_____

_____

Your goals and objectives for priority publics: What do you want them to do for your school?

Public: _____

Goals of communication effort: _____

Public: _____

Goals of communication effort: _____

Public: _____

Goals of communication effort: _____

Public: _____

Goals of communication effort: _____

Public: _____

Goals of communication effort: _____

Step 3: **Research**

Conduct focus groups or interviews of your targeted audiences (publics) to learn more about their perceptions of your school and the best ways to communicate with them; seek their assistance in making your communication plan a winner.

Step 4: **Messages/Content**

List general information that is important for audiences to know — calendar, special events, lunch menu, etc.

_____   _____

_____   _____

_____   _____

_____   _____

_____   _____

_____   _____

Now, by target audience, list key messages that will help you reach your goals.

Public   **Message**

_____   _____

_____   _____

_____   _____

_____   _____

_____   _____

_____   _____

_____   _____

_____   _____

_____   _____

_____   _____

_____   _____

_____   _____

_____   _____

_____   _____

Step 5: *Tactics*

List the tactics you plan to implement during the next year. Be sure to mix mass communication techniques (newsletters, brochures) and interpersonal communication techniques (meetings, forums, discussion groups).

Tactic: _____

Audience	Message	Time line	Responsibility
_____	_____	_____	_____
_____	_____	_____	_____
_____	_____	_____	_____
_____	_____	_____	_____
_____	_____	_____	_____

Step 6: *Keeping on target*

Follow the maxim, *What gets measured gets done.* Keep the plan alive by reviewing key dates at staff or site council meetings.

Step 7: *Crisis communication plan*

This is an important step that you cannot overlook. One of the quickest ways of losing support for your school is to mismanage a crisis. Make sure your current plan is up to date.

Step 8: *Evaluation*

Go back to the focus groups to see how this year's program met audience communication needs.

- Did the target audiences do what you expected them to do?

Begin revising your plan for next year.

Planning for a crisis

Section 4 deals with communication tools and techniques. It closes with important guidelines for creating a crisis plan for your school.

Remember that all of your ongoing efforts to engage the public and build support can easily be wiped out by a mismanaged crisis. Many times, the reputation of schools are not blemished by a crises, but by the way the crisis was managed.

Communication plays a large role in handling a crisis, so prepare now for a day that we all hope will never happen.

Effective Communication
Tools & Techniques

Effective Communication

In this section, you'll find some ideas and tools for communicating with your most important audiences — parents, staff, and the news media. You'll also find some ideas and tools for dealing with your school's reputation and the thing that can damage that most quickly — a crisis.

Communicating with and Engaging Parents

One of the most important audiences for any school is its parents. They have an everyday interest in what occurs at your school and they make major decisions that can affect your school, such as whether their students remain enrolled there or not. Other community members also see parents as credible sources of information.

For these reasons, you should be especially sensitive to the communication needs of parents. Make sure that you have appropriate channels in place to communicate with them.

Some communication opportunities occur in all schools. Among these are:

    1. parent-teacher conferences,

    2. newsletters,

    3. comments from teachers that students bring home, and

    4. PTA or booster club meetings.

Principals face two challenges in parent communication — making the best use of these typical opportunities and creating additional opportunities to meet the special needs of their school and its parents. Here are some ideas to keep in mind:

❖ **Communicate with parents now.** Many times teachers and others at your school need support from parents to correct problems, such as tardiness, disrespect for others, or lack of preparation for class. Parents will more readily provide that support if they have received positive communication from your school before they hear that their youngster has problems.

➤ Idea for Action:  Some teachers prepare and mail letters to all parents at the start of each school year to introduce themselves and their class and to outline their expectations for the year.

Parents also tend to feel more positive when they are encouraged to call their children's teachers whenever they have a question, and the teacher's home telephone number is included in the letter.

➤ Idea for Action:  Teachers at one school visit each of their students at home in late August. This practice allows them to meet their students and parents on their own turf and to learn more about them.

Conducting home visits before the school year begins can have contractual implications, but they are an investment in subsequent success for teachers. They certainly deliver a message that the teacher cares.

❖ ***Share the good news.*** When students do well, let their parents know. You can do this through phone calls, happygrams, postcards, or letters. The important thing is to get this information home. Praise students for all successes, including improved attendance or better effort. Don't recognize students only for earning straight A's.

➤ Idea for Action: Phone calls home are great opportunities for teachers to not only share good news about students, but also to receive positive comments in return. If some teachers resist making such calls, ask three energetic teachers to try this idea.

Encourage them to identify five students during each of the next three months and make positive phone calls to their parents. Typically, the parents are so happy to receive these calls that they commend the teachers for their initiative.

If this practice works well, give the three teachers time at a staff meeting to talk about their experience; they are likely to motivate others to try this idea.

❖ ***Provide the information that parents want and need.*** You can probably anticipate these topics — grading policy, homework requirements, discipline policy, and ways to contact the teacher.

If you are unclear about which topics to include or if you want to ensure that you've covered everything, simply ask a few key parents.

You can disseminate the information in any number of ways — in parent handbooks, letters from the teacher, during Back-to-School night meetings, and on calendars.

Be sure to include the really important information more than once and in more than one format. People frequently need to see something more than once to remember it.

❖ **Remember diversity**. Schools today usually have parents who speak languages other than English. If large numbers of your school's parent population do not speak English, make every effort to communicate important information in other languages.

Meet with parent leaders of those groups to determine the best approach for that population. (See *6: Communication in a Diverse World* for more information about this topic.)

❖ **Recognize parents.** It's tough being a parent today, and many dedicated parents go unrecognized. Frankly, schools need highly motivated parents working with them to provide the best possible opportunities for students.

Education benefits when principals include parents on the list of those to be nurtured and recognized.

❖ **Involve parents.** Many parents want to be involved and schools should welcome that participation. In the past, many schools felt that the staff were the experts and everyone else should stay away. Today, many parents are involved as classroom aides, as members of site councils, as tutors, and in other ways.

When principals encourage parent involvement, not only do they get additional help, but they also provide a way for an important audience to see first-hand the accomplishments of the school. Once you have that help, it's important to recognize it.

Here are some tips to consider:

❖ ***Make the work worthwhile.*** It's a big mistake to encourage people to volunteer in your school and then not give them important ways to become a part of your school team. This lack of follow-through may be seen as a slap in the face to some people, certainly the opposite of positive recognition.

❖ ***Teach parenting skills.*** Train parents how to handle the various challenges that they face today. This training can range from how to teach your child arithmetic skills to how to study more effectively or how to identify early signs of drug experimentation.

Schools can provide multi-week parenting classes one night a week, or they can offer single workshops. The more you can do to help parents do their job better, the easier your school's job will be.

❖ ***Hold a Parent Day***. Some elementary schools schedule a Parent Day once a year when students bring their parents to the school for the day. Parents can see first-hand what occurs at school, and the principal, teachers, and others have ample opportunity to thank parents for their efforts.

There's always more than enough work to do in any school today — both in the classroom and in the office. So, any school should value a number of talented, dedicated volunteers.

One way to make sure that volunteers remain committed to your school is by recognizing their efforts. Again, saying thank you is a great start, but here are some other ideas principals use:

❖ **Volunteer luncheon.** End the year with a luncheon for all your volunteers. Invite local businesses to contribute prizes for drawings. Have a good high school foods class prepare and serve the lunch. It's a great way to wrap up the year for volunteers and urge them to be back next year.

❖ **Thank-you letters.** You can always write thank-you notes, but notes are frequently more appreciated if they come from students. Encourage elementary school teachers to have their students write thank-you notes to the volunteers who have helped them during the year.

❖ **Special events.** Invite volunteers to join you for special ceremonies at the school, even if it's not part of their volunteer time. Events might include the Thanksgiving dinner or holiday celebration at your school. These invitations tell volunteers you appreciate them.

➤ Idea for Action: One principal has a postcard headed, *"There are 10 reasons why we like you. Here's one:"* The principal makes sure that each volunteer receives that postcard once or twice a year with a personally written note.

> There are 10 reasons why
> we like you. Here's one:

 Parent Involvement Can Be Fun

Although parent involvement has more to do with a child's success in school than any other factor, involving parents is not easy. Sure, most of our schools have parent-teacher organizations, parent advisory councils, and similar groups, but these usually include only a small number of parents — and often the same ones serve on several committees. Studies show that many more parents would like to participate but are too busy, too tired, or too stressed to do so.

How, then, do you get large numbers of parents to be regularly involved with your school? In addition to placing parents in advisory or decision-making roles, it's also important to plan fun activities. For example, we have found that parents will flock to our school to see their children perform or to participate in activities with them.

How do you go about planning these activities?

❖ The first step is to establish a parent involvement committee that includes several teachers, a small, diverse group of interested parents, and the principal. The committee's goal should be to brainstorm a number of enjoyable activities for parents that are simple and easy to implement.

❖ Once the committee produces a list of possible activities, staff members should be allowed to select those that they feel most comfortable implementing. For example, a teacher who might feel intimidated by having parents in the classroom could select evening activities. Each teacher and the principal should prepare

time frames for scheduled parent activities. These plans are then listed and combined into a composite schedule so any required equipment and facilities can be identified and reserved.

The composite schedule is necessary to ensure that two or more activities aren't scheduled for the same time and location. It also allows you to spread the activities over the school year. Ideally, there should be at least one activity each month, giving parents a number of opportunities to visit the school.

❖ Now all you have left to do is to invite parents to attend the various activities. Teachers can send invitations home with their students or notify parents of upcoming events through their class newsletters. You can also use the school's newsletter or a special bulletin board in the lobby to list the month's schedule of parent activities. If your school has access to a local cable channel, take advantage of it to get the word out. Whatever means of communication you use, it is essential that parents know about all upcoming events.

We have successfully developed and implemented a number of enjoyable parent activities at our school. Here are several examples that may help your school get started:

❖ ***Dessert Social.*** During the second week of school, we invite parents and children to attend an informal evening event and taste desserts donated by volunteers. This activity gives parents a chance to mingle and chat with the principal, teachers, and one another in the school cafeteria.

❖ ***Listeners' Corner.*** We invite parents of primary-level students to visit their classrooms one day a week to hear their children read aloud. Teachers coordinate this activity

so that three or four students get an opportunity to read in front of the class for five minutes each with their parents present. This activity takes only 15 to 20 minutes, and each student gets a chance to read over a five-week period. We give parents several weeks' notice before their child is scheduled to read, so they can get time off from work, if necessary.

❖ *Game Day.* Teachers invite parents to play educational games, such as chess, checkers or Scrabble, in the classrooms with their children. At our school, this activity is held once a month on Friday afternoon for the last 45 minutes of the day.

❖ *D.A.R.E.* We invite parents to sit in on our Drug Abuse Resistance Education classes, which are held once a week for 17 weeks and are coordinated by classroom teachers and the D.A.R.E. police officer assigned to the school.

❖ *Family Fun Night.* Parents and children are invited to participate in scooter races, sack races, and relay races at this winter evening activity in the gym. It's strictly for fun — no prizes are awarded.

❖ *Mother's Day Luncheon.* Students' mothers are invited by the teachers to come to school on the Friday before Mother's Day and have lunch in the classroom, where they sit at students' desks and are waited on by their children. The PTA might purchase platters, or the luncheon might consist of sandwiches provided by the teacher or parent volunteers. Teachers can also prepare a short program in which students recite Mother's Day poems and sing songs.

❖ ***Writing Fair.*** We invite parents and children to attend an evening writing fair each spring. Writing samples are displayed on tables and walls, giving parents an opportunity to see finished pieces that their children have written. This is an informal event and no awards are presented.

As you can see from this sample of planned activities, we have succeeded in developing a parent involvement program emphasizing activities that are fun, non-threatening, easy to implement — and well-attended. More than 100 parents annually attend our dessert social, more than 300 come to the writing fair, and we have had excellent turnouts for many other activities.

In developing parent involvement activities, the focus should be on planning events that are fun for everyone — parents, children, teachers, and the principal.

Remember that involvement can take many different forms, so be creative in planning enjoyable activities. Open the doors to your school and have some fun!

Richard P. Grandmont
Principal
Manchester (Ct.)
From the March 1997 issue of *Principal*

Communicating with School Staff

The greatest resource any school has for building support in the community is its staff. Unfortunately, that staff can also harm the school's reputation if it is uninformed or poorly motivated.

Consider how many times each week your staff talks about your school — as secretaries respond to questions on the telephone, as teachers hold conferences with parents, as bus drivers chat with parents at the bus stop, and as every person on your staff talks with family, neighbors, and friends.

Every time staff members are questioned about schools, they have an opportunity to make people aware of your school successes or to answer questions about your school's effectiveness. It's essential that staff contacts with the community build support, not raise more questions. As the reputation leader of the school, you must motivate all your staff to take advantage of these opportunities.

Part of your task, then, is to:

❖ Explain that effective communication and public relations has an important outcome for all members of your school staff — *greater community support,*

❖ Provide staff development on public relations skills, and

❖ Make sure that all staff members have up-to-date, accurate information about your school, especially about staff, student, and program successes.

In developing an effective plan for staff communication, it's imperative that you understand who the frequent sources of information are. In surveys conducted in community after community, support staff tops that list.

Support staff tops the list of frequent sources of information.

Research shows that:

- ❖ secretaries,
- ❖ custodians,
- ❖ bus drivers, and
- ❖ cafeteria workers

provide the most information to the general public. Following these four groups are:

- ❖ classroom aides,
- ❖ teachers,
- ❖ school building administrators, and
- ❖ central office administrators.

These data should show you the value of informing your support staff about *all* important school decisions, including those dealing with the curriculum. A custodian who doesn't understand why a new reading program has been implemented — which involves lots more student interaction and, therefore, more noise in the classrooms — could conclude and tell his friends that the program's a waste of money. That sentiment will erode support for your next tax election and harm the reputation of your school.

Understanding the importance of staff communication, you must find the best ways to deliver messages to all members of your staff. While staff bulletins are a traditional means, research shows that most employees like to receive information in small meetings from their immediate supervisor.

Most employees like to receive information in small meetings from their immediate supervisor.

Although schools have different staffing structures, remember the importance of having immediate supervisors inform their staff members. You should establish communication plans to reflect this research, especially for those important times, such as bond or finance

campaigns, curriculum or organizational changes, and decisions that are likely to be widely discussed in your community.

Communicating with specific staff audiences

Once you have plans in place to inform all staff about your school and its successes, communication by staff must be *two-way*. That is, staff members must share this school and district information with students, parents, community members, and other key audiences, and *they must be willing listeners to those people's reactions*.

Make sure that your school's communication processes encourage this feedback and enable it to occur.

The rest of this section focuses on specific ideas for several staff audiences, including:

❖ teachers,

❖ substitute teachers,

❖ secretaries, and

❖ other support staff.

Some of these ideas are cited for a single group, but can be used for many.

Teachers

Motivating teachers and cheering them on

Staff Bulletin. The staff bulletin is another traditional means of communication. Its key advantage is that everyone receives the information at the same time and in the same language. It records new policies and directions and people can refer to it in the future. You should publish the staff bulletin consistently and distribute it to *all* staff — teachers and support.

➤ Idea for Action:

Staff bulletins are a great way to share the achievements of your school and the people in it. Consider having a section in each newsletter where teachers or other staff members can brag about what their students are doing. Have staff members write this column.

❖ **Writing Weekly Bulletins for Staff**

A short way into my 20-year sojourn as a principal, I found that keeping myself organized was not the unattainable goal I once feared. It was keeping everyone else organized that was the challenge. I discovered that just performing their normal duties requires a lot of planning for our staff members. Add in numerous meetings, events, and special assignments, and there's even more to keep track of.

I have learned to rely on specific and frequent communication to disseminate information and help my teachers stay organized. The cornerstone of this communication effort is a weekly bulletin that is short, easy to read, and loaded with the essential information they need to navigate through a busy week.

Format

I use a basic word-processing program to compose the bulletin, making each item a brief "quick read" and limiting the bulletin to both sides of a single sheet of paper.

At the top of each bulletin is the title, date, and school name. I highlight key items by enclosing them with borders, setting them in different fonts and type sizes, and by using bullets and check-off lists.

I organize the bulletin information — everything from student club meetings to inservice news—under the following headings:

❖ ***This Week:*** I list, day by day, all activities scheduled for the week. Under Monday, for example, I might note a social committee meeting before school, a migrant health screening at 10:30 and a student concert at 7:00 p.m. I also use this section to alert staff to changes in the school routine, such as an early dismissal or a revised recess time. It is critical that each week's listing be complete and that all dates and times are accurate. If you list the awards assembly at the wrong time, have the wrong day for the third-grade field trip, or omit Grandparents' Day, both you and your bulletin lose credibility.

❖ ***Due:*** This is one of the most helpful services the bulletin provides. Using a check-off format, I list items that are due to me, the secretary, and the district office. These include personnel forms, supply orders, and program surveys. I also list weekly or monthly assignments, such as which classes are scheduled to clean up the playground or which teachers are responsible for filling the office display case with student art.

❖ **Upcoming events:** This list of dates and events forewarns staff about activities coming up in the next 4 to 6 weeks, such as committee meetings, assemblies, concerts, and field trips. I include times and locations as soon as they are available to aid in advance planning. Eventually, these events will show up in *This Week*.

❖ **Social news:** Staff celebrations, get-togethers, and birthday parties are highlighted here, including information about committee responsibilities, potluck menus, and gift donations.

❖ **General information:** Here is where I place miscellaneous items, such as the custodian's new mowing schedule or the cook's menu changes. I also include messages for teachers to read to students, such as a warning about a playground hazard or a reminder about the dress code. This is where to look for PTO policy decisions, school budget status reports, and classroom fund-raising plans.

❖ **News you can use:** I devote this portion of the bulletin to a potpourri of tidbits aimed at professional growth — an uplifting quote, a book synopsis, or information about an upcoming workshop. I also let teachers know about their colleagues' innovative activities. For example: "*Theme Idea*: Sue's class is integrating writing, math, and science in its exploration of the Iditarod dogsled race. Check out the student maps and displays outside her room."

❖ *Humor:*   I leave space at the bottom of the page for a favorite cartoon, a whimsical anecdote, or a funny quote.

Production and distribution

I write the bulletin on Friday, using the previous issue as a template, and I have my secretary proofread it for errors before making copies. I arrange for copies to be put in faculty mailboxes on Monday morning. I also provide copies for all staff members and district administrators.

Although the teachers have electronic mailboxes, I don't send the bulletin by e-mail. I have discovered that while teachers check their office mailboxes daily, many delay reading their e-mail, sometimes for days. I have also found that teachers like to save the bulletin for future reference, and some find that printing out e-mail is a nuisance.

Supplementing the bulletin

I don't rely solely on the weekly bulletin to keep everyone well-informed and up to date. When there is late-breaking news, a sudden change in plans, or a particularly important event, I supplement the bulletin with intercom announcements and electronic newsbreaks.

❖ *Intercom announcements*: At the start of each day, I use the intercom to remind students and teachers about that day's events, including a brief, historical tidbit, such as: "On this day in 1863, President Lincoln delivered the Gettysburg Address."

❖ *Electronic newsbreaks*: I might use the schools' e-mail network to announce the birth of a staff member's baby, a teacher's recruitment plan, or a meeting time change. If you don't have e-mail in your building, these late-breaking news items can be included in half-sheet supplemental bulletins and placed in staff mailboxes.

I've found that a comprehensive and concise weekly bulletin — supplemented with daily announcements and occasional electronic updates — gives teachers the information and reminders they need. It may lack glamor, but it yields two immeasurable rewards — well-informed and dependable employees, and a smooth-running school.

Cathie E. West
Principal
East Wenatchee (Wa.)

From the September 1997 issue of *Principal*

 ### *You Can Make a Difference*

In many ways the principal's motivational role is really that of a cheerleader, vocalizing encouragement and praise. All teachers respond to praise, and one of my most effective motivational strategies was to distribute throughout the district a bulletin headlined, *You Can Make a Difference.* In it I listed at least one positive contribution that year from every one of our teachers. It was appreciated not only by our teachers, but those from other schools in the district, who called to thank me for recognizing the efforts of their peers.

A principal can do many other things to motivate staff members, but none of them will work unless the principal is motivated—and the staff is aware of it.

Here are some tips:

❖ The first meeting of the year is an excellent time to communicate your enthusiasm to teachers. It can be contagious!

❖ Don't use the same old format for the school bulletin year after year, changing only the dates and a few names. This gives staff members a not-so-subtle message: *Everything is the same; nothing has changed.*

❖ Reward deserving teachers. A reward need be no more elaborate than a pat on the back, or a principal saying, *When I passed your room the other day, I saw that your kids were really wrapped up and involved with the lesson you were working on. Keep it up!*

❖ A personal note from the principal placed in a teacher's mailbox can be a good motivating tool. Or you may prefer to use a computer to create and personalize certificates of recognition for staff members. *A word of caution:* Don't be overly effusive with your praise. Insincere compliments lose their significance.

❖ An excellent improvement incentive for mediocre teachers is to assign them whenever possible to classes they have expressed a desire to teach.

❖ Allow interested teachers to attend professional meetings and conventions. I've never been to one from which I didn't come away with at least one good idea.

❖ Designate a choice reserved parking spot and award it each month to a staff member for a significant achievement.

❖ Never verbally reprimand a teacher in public. Even if the censure is deserved, it will create resentment in the teacher and fear in others, effectively negating any attempts at motivation.

❖ Never promise and then fail to deliver! If you tell a teacher that you're going to do something, then do it. Don't be wishy-washy. Make decisions as wisely as possible and then abide by them.

❖ Make a concerted effort to know your faculty on a more personal basis. We talk about getting to know the whole child and we should do the same for our teachers. The more that we share their good times and their not-so-good times, both inside and outside of school, the better our chances of being able to understand them and to help them become better teachers.

James W. Jeffries
Principal
Granite City, (Il.)

From the January 1994 issue of *Principal*

Other ideas from NAESP's resources include:

❖ Idaho's Pamela Pratt kicks off the school year by giving a T-shirt printed with a catchy school message to every employee, from cook to counselor. Then she gives out a few "110%" pins and classy certificates for staffers who performed a good deed over the summer.

❖ Trophies are awarded to three staffers each September by Lillian Tafoya at her California elementary school. The awards celebrate over-the-summer school activities, such as painting lockers or organizing files. "Then these three identify three more staff who keep the Hall of Fame growing," she says.

❖ In Nevada, Peggy Moore provides *Good Egg* awards for staff to give one another. She also writes to parents, enclosing three recognition forms they can use to thank special teachers for their extra efforts. A *Teacher Feature* during assemblies points out jobs well done; the PTA celebrates teacher birthdays by donating a book to the library. "Teacher Appreciation Week is a big blowout around here," says Moore, who praises from morning (every faculty meeting begins with a thank-you) to night (with e-mail messages from her home computer).

❖ At Nancy Krodel's Oklahoma school, teachers formed a book club. Kordel buys children's books and provides the refreshments for monthly meetings. Not only do teachers learn new ways to present literature to students, but they enjoy each other in a different setting.

❖ Every spring in North Carolina, Trossie Wall rewards teachers and builds *esprit de corps* with a two-day, overnight inservice led by local university staff. In Tennessee, Martha Jean Bratton's staff enjoys a weekend of

renewal and inservice at a nearby resort. Nationally known consultants are hired and partial expenses are paid by the school.

❖ California's Lillian Tafoya, like her nationally recognized colleagues, makes her feedback specific. "I write little notes that say something like, 'As I walked through your classroom today, I observed that the children were all on task,' or 'That's the best science lesson I've seen.'" Some rewards at this school, which serves impoverished children, are in cash. Each teacher gets a $25 shopping spree to buy "goodies" for students, mainly for positive reinforcement. Others of Tafoya's honors are edible. She draws names and sends baskets of cookies baked by the cafeteria just for teachers.

❖ By the end of the school year in California, Tafoya's school office is plastered with signs of recognition. "We hang a banner whenever we can, for new babies, new staff, engagements, marriages, contest winners," she says, "and we leave them there all year." She also alerts the press to good deeds. "I send out press releases as often as I can, I want everyone to know the good attitudes, commitment, and enthusiasm of my staff." That's good for morale—and great PR.

June Million
Public Information Director
NAESP

From the December 1995 issue of *Communicator*

Delivering Information

Communicate with parents. While there's nothing new about this, nothing can replace positive communication from teachers to parents about their youngster. Whether it's through phone calls, written notes, postcards, or happygrams, parents appreciate hearing good things about their kids.

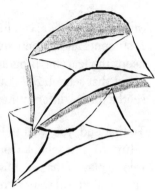

This communication motivates the student, encourages parental involvement, and sets the foundation for times when teachers must ask parents for help in correcting problems.

If this practice has not been the mode in your school in the past, ask two or three energetic teachers to try it on a pilot basis. Usually, they will receive so much thanks from parents that they will motivate the remainder of the faculty to make the contacts.

Try home visits. Ask teachers to visit the homes of incoming students during the late summer. It's helpful to get to know the parents and students on "their turf." Yes, this takes time and the practice may have contractual implications, but it also delivers a strong message to parents that teachers care. The visit will make the teacher's job easier during the remainder of the year.

In some communities, you may want to have visits in a nearby community center or church hall. Some parents may not feel comfortable having you visit in their homes.

Substitute Teachers

Substitute teachers can make a school look either great or weak. If students and parents see that a substitute steps right in and keeps the learning program going, they will have a positive view about that school. But if an entire day is filled with videos, you send a totally different message.

To that end, you want to have the best substitutes wanting to return to your school. Communication and public relations has a role to play in that. A substitute who is informed and feels appreciated will want to return.

Receiving Information

Set clear expectations. Make sure that substitutes have a clear idea of what you expect of them in the classroom and make sure that the regular staff prepares adequate lesson plans. The principal, or the assistant principals and department heads in larger schools, should meet with each new substitute as soon as that person arrives. Make certain that you meet the needs of the new substitute.

Demonstrate your interest. The principal or assistant principal should try to stop by the substitute's classroom during first hour. A few minutes can demonstrate that you care and can also assure you that the day has begun well.

➤ Idea for Action:

A new substitute can feel lonely and without a friend since he or she is likely not to know members of the staff. Take a Polaroid photo of the sub at the start of the day and post it with some basic information in a special section of the staff lounge. That way the regular teachers can greet the sub during breaks and at lunch.

Delivering Information

Cultivate credibility. The public is likely to perceive substitutes as being very credible sources of information about your school. They have first-hand experience at your school, but are not part of the regular staff. Community members frequently ask substitutes questions about a school months after that sub has worked in the school. Let subs know that they are always welcome to ask questions about your school's operation so that they can accurately answer questions in the community.

➤ Idea for Action: Send substitutes who have done a good job for you the staff bulletin and any other publications, such as school calendars or data on your achievements, that will keep them informed about the school. They will see that you care about them, and they will be more likely to want to return to your school. Also, they'll answer questions more accurately.

*I*n most communities, the secretary is the number one source of information about the school.

Secretaries

In most communities, the secretary is the number one source of information about the school for the community at large. Thus, the secretary has a tremendous role in establishing your school's reputation.

Receiving Information

Keep them informed. Keep all secretaries well-informed about new decisions, new areas of emphasis in classrooms and elsewhere, and personnel changes. Some principals schedule a 10-minute coffee break with their secretary each morning to discuss such items. That way, the secretary is prepared to respond to questions

from any audience, and the secretary will understand that he or she is a valued member of your staff.

Say thanks. An appreciated secretary is a motivated secretary. Be certain that secretaries understand how important they are. Remembering to say thank you, occasionally bringing them a cup of coffee, and sending cards on special occasions will all add up.

➤ Idea for Action:

Be creative on Secretaries Day, and continue that creativity throughout the year. Sure, flowers are nice, but a little extra thinking will demonstrate how highly you regard your secretaries.

Some principals give their secretary a gift certificate for two to a restaurant for dinner. Others encourage a student foods class to prepare a lunch for all the secretaries, with the principal answering the phones during that time.

Delivering Information

Ask for communication ideas. Any secretary delivers a great deal of information by simply answering the telephone. However, the creative principal-secretary team that wants to strengthen the school's reputation will look for additional ways to communicate.

➤ Idea for Action:

Give your secretary the responsibility — not just the job — of evaluating your communication to parents and other community members. This includes reviewing letters, memos, and newsletter messages. Frequently the secretary is a longtime member of the community who knows how others react to what is written. This is a valuable service secretaries can provide and will help them understand how important they are.

Other Support Staff

Custodians, bus drivers, food service staff, classroom aides, and others are all important people in your school family, and they are very credible communicators. Many reside in the community and are seen as sources of accurate information about your school. Plus, they deal with students each day.

Receiving Information

Keep them informed. It's essential to provide complete information about your school to all staff, including the support staff. Custodians, bus drivers, and others will be asked questions about safety in your school, new instructional programs, the quality of kids, and much more. And they won't hesitate to answer these questions. Send these individuals the staff newsletter, the school handbook, and other publications.

Remember the support staff when it comes to staff meetings. If it's impossible to include them in regular staff meetings, schedule special meetings when it is appropriate. A science teacher or student could explain a new aspect of the science curriculum at such a meeting.

➤ Idea for Action: Institute a *Time for Support Staff* when any support staff member can come to your office to discuss anything. This could be a monthly event.

➤ Idea for Action: Encourage the student council or some other student group to plan a *Celebrate Our Support Staff Day* when the kids create activities to recognize and thank the support staff. They could bring them apples, do their jobs for a portion of the day, give them thank-you cards, or develop any number of other creative ideas.

Delivering Information

Sometimes support staff believe that all they are supposed to do is clean the classroom or cook the food. There's so much more they can do, and you should encourage them to become active in developing a positive reputation for your school.

> **Give your support staff a PR role.** It makes sense to hold a professional development session on public relations for professional support staff. They should learn that effective PR leads to community support for the school, how people form attitudes, and specific PR skills. (NSPRA's *School Communication Workshop Kit* is a good resource for this.)

> **Be role models for kids.** Urge support staff to develop positive relationships with students. After all, the bus driver is the first and last school person many students see each day.

> ➤ Idea for Action:  Urge bus drivers to develop *Bus Rider of the Month* certificates to present to elementary school students. It's a twist to the happygram, and allows bus drivers to recognize young people.

Always remember that your school staff must be the foundation of any effective communication program. Or, as some people say, *Remember to go in-house before you go out-house.*

Or, in the words of Thomas R. Martin of Federal Express Corporation,

> **I've never understood why some companies will gladly spend millions touting their services to customers, but spend next-to-nothing communicating to employees who deliver those services.**

Communicating with the News Media

Do you dream at night about television cameras descending on your campus? In these nightmares, do all reporters have one large eyeball in the middle of their forehead and are they salivating?

Those impressions should not dictate your relationships with the news media in your community. News media relations have a role to play in any public relations program, and those relationships can be positive for you.

How you approach the news media is the key.

All communities have news outlets — daily newspapers, weekly newspapers, television and radio stations, magazines, and specialty publications. You won't find all of these in every community, but you'll usually find some of them. In addition, if your school faces a crisis, you are likely to have to deal with state and the national news media, including wire services, national newspapers, and even the sensational television news shows.

If you understand how to work with reporters and if you know some strategies to become more assertive with the news media, you'll be able to deliver your message more effectively and, at the same time, stay out of hot water.

This section begins with some general guidelines, as well as specific ideas that you can use to have an impact on news coverage and discusses dealing with the electronic press.

Basic Guidelines for Working with the News Media

Educators need to realize that reporters, editors, and news directors are not your school's public relations department. Making you look good is not their job. However, if you provide them with ideas and materials about positive activities at your school, and if you do it in the right way, positive coverage can result.

Help with news media relations may be available through your district office if a public relations professional is on staff. If so, that's the place to start.

❖ **Different school systems have different practices regarding their school's responsibilities in media relations.** Some large school systems encourage individual schools to submit news releases directly to the local media; others prefer that information be sent to the district office which prepares and disseminates releases. Some school districts even provide media training for their principals and others. Your district probably has Board policies relating to media relations, including guidelines for allowing television cameras onto school grounds. If your school district has a PR professional, be sure to discuss these policies and practices with that person.

❖ **Whenever possible, get to know the reporters who cover schools.** Many newspapers have education reporters, while radio and television stations probably do not. Certainly, getting to know reporters takes time, but it's part of your investment in PR. Since the best resource you have when dealing with reporters is the credibility you have already established with them, you need to get to know them before a crisis occurs.

Read the papers to see who reports on education. Invite that person to your school. Have in mind some of the good programs at your school that might interest the reporter, but don't expect a story to automatically result from this first meeting.

Read the papers to see who reports on education.

At this point, your main objective should be to establish a relationship in which the reporter views you as honest, objective, willing to talk, and willing to see your story covered. This is also a good time to discuss the reporter's

needs, including deadlines and the way the reporter prefers to receive ideas. Sharing a few ideas for future stories and stating that you would be happy to have the reporter talk to students and staff for the stories is a good strategy for the future.

❖ **One effective way to build relationships with reporters and editors is to involve them in your school.** A reporter could lecture a Language Arts class, a radio personality could be the emcee for a school dance, editors could talk to younger students about journalism as a career, media outlets could host tours of their facilities, or reporters could speak at your school about current issues in the community. Establishing a relationship now will reward you for years in the future.

What the Media Can Do for You

❖ **Working with the news media is valuable.** A good, front-page article certainly will not solve all your communication problems, but you can reap positive outcomes from it. To set realistic expectations, you need to understand what news coverage will and won't do for you.

Some audiences pay close attention to the media, including business leaders, legislators, and other opinion leaders. Naturally, the attitudes these people hold are important to your school, and coverage in the press — especially editorial coverage — will catch their attention. However, don't think that news coverage by itself will change attitudes. News coverage and other mass communication activities can make people aware of an idea and build their interest in it. However, that coverage is not likely to make people act.

Also, the news media is effective in reaching a large number of people, both quickly and fairly inexpensively, such as when school is closed due to snow or another emergency. However, those stations are not the best vehicles for convincing people to send their youngsters to your school.

Your task is to work well with the news media in those areas where they can help you reach your public relations goals.

How Can You Get Coverage?

One of the first questions to ask is, "What is news?" This is somewhat like asking, "What is a good book?" A story idea that has great appeal to one editor may come across as a real yawner to another. However, there are some general guidelines you can follow.

❖ **News is different, timely, new, unusual, and affects a large number of people.** For example, the first time your school hosts a Senior Prom for senior citizens — that is different and new. There's a good chance that newspapers and television stations may cover this event since it's unusual. The 25th Annual Thanksgiving Picnic in the fourth grade classroom, however, isn't likely to get coverage unless an editor is looking for a Thanksgiving photo — it has happened before. It's positive, but it's not *news*.

❖ **Timeliness is important.** If a major event is occurring at your school, it's news ***now***, not three weeks from now. For scheduled events, such as the governor speaking to your elementary school students, let reporters know in advance so they can consider the idea and plan coverage if they're interested. Knowing how far in advance you need to give a reporter information is one of the questions to ask during your initial meeting. However, a good guideline is that you should contact the media:

✔ two days before the event for daily newspapers,
✔ a week before for weekly newspapers, and
✔ a day before for radio and television.

When you report results of an event, such as the winner of your school geography bee, get that information to the news media as soon as possible after the event. Mailing a news release two weeks after the event makes

this *old news*, and the event is not likely to be reported. Faxing or phoning the information immediately increases your chances of coverage tremendously.

If you want media coverage for your school, always keep an eye open for instructional programs that are newsworthy.

Reporters and Mistakes

Since journalists are human beings, they make mistakes like the rest of us. Unfortunately, however, their mistakes are frequently communicated to large numbers of people. If you find that a reporter has erred in reporting about you, you should act, but always in a positive, professional manner.

First evaluate just how severe the mistake is, and base your action on that evaluation. If the newspaper reporter misspelled your name, that is not as major as reporting that test scores at your school were 15 points lower than they actually are.

All mistakes should be discussed, if only so the reporter will be accurate the next time. Ask for corrective action, such as a printed correction, only if the issue has a serious impact on your school's reputation.

Just as principals suggest to parents that they start with the teacher if a problem arises in the classroom, so should you start with the reporter. Here's what you should do:

❖ Explain what the mistake is and what impact it has had.

❖ Take the time to make sure the reporter leaves the conversation with a complete understanding of the issue; some education issues can be hard to understand.

❖ If the reporter refuses to talk with you about an error or consistently reports inaccurately, meet with the reporter's supervisor. At newspapers, that would be a city editor or the editor of smaller papers. At television and radio stations, it usually would be the assignment editor.

Some Other Golden Rules

One key concept to keep in mind is that reporters always work under deadlines. You don't have to drop everything when they call, but if you want your comments to be included in a story, you must talk to a reporter before their deadline.

Remember, reporters always work under deadlines.

When reporters call and you cannot speak with them at that time, or you need time to collect data to respond accurately, ask when their deadlines are and promise to get back to them before then. If you always follow through, you'll build credibility.

❖ *It's unwise to use the phrase, "No comment."* To many reporters and readers, saying, "No comment," *is* a comment and suggests that you have something to hide. When you are prohibited from discussing an issue, such as a student's record, explain why you are precluded from talking about it. Try to be as open and honest as possible — doing so will build your credibility with reporters and will help get the coverage you desire in the long run.

❖ *Another term to be wary of is "off the record."* It's good advice never to speak "off the record" unless you would trust the reporter with your job and you have a specific purpose in mind. Before commenting, get the reporter to agree that the conversation will be off the record. Better yet, just don't do it at all.

Look for ways to initiate coverage that will communicate your messages.

Strategic Media Relations

As with any aspect of public relations, you'll be able to deal successfully with the news media if you approach your task in a strategic, planned fashion. It is unwise to simply wait for reporters to descend upon your school; you should look for ways to initiate coverage that will communicate your messages.

You may also choose to keep your central office informed about your media relations activities so that they may be able to help you. It is also beneficial for the central office to know when principals are working with the media to prevent 30 principals from sending in an Op-Ed piece on the same issue. (If 30 principals write the same Op-Ed piece, yours will probably not run.)

Here are some specific opportunities you may create:

❖ ***Op-Ed articles*** —Many newspapers— large and small — print Op-Ed or opinion articles as part of their editorial section. Op-Ed articles express opinions and are written by someone who is not on the newspaper's staff.

In your community paper, you might find that the president of the Realty Board, the mayor, or a spokesperson from a citizens organization has written an Op-Ed article. Remember, that opportunity also exists for you or someone else associated with your school.

Look to see if your newspaper publishes Op-Ed articles. If so, call the paper and ask to speak with the person in charge of them. Large newspapers usually have an editor of the editorial page; on smaller papers, it's probably the editor who is in charge of the Op-Ed section.

❖ ***Suggest a topic for an Op-Ed article*** and ask for the chance to submit it. Never ask for a guarantee that it will be used, only for the opportunity to submit it.

❖ ***Find out the appropriate length*** and any other information you'll need. Then write the article in a crisp, clear style, forgetting all the education jargon you have ever learned.

❖ ***Submit the article with a cover letter thanking the editor*** for the opportunity and include a one- or two-sentence description of the author. You may want to submit the article "exclusively" to one newspaper. That means you will not send it anywhere else until the first paper decides it does not want to use it. A typical strategy is to submit such an article

exclusively to the largest newspaper in the area. If that paper refuses it, you can then submit it to the second largest.

Keep trying until you find some paper that will use the piece. Be sure to let the paper know it has the article on an exclusive basis, but that you would like to know its status as soon as a decision is made so that you can send it elsewhere if that paper doesn't print it.

❖ **You can mail, FAX, or deliver the article.** Some people feel that sending it by FAX attaches more urgency to the article.

It is appropriate to make one follow-up call to verify that the article has been received, but do not pester editors with call after call. They, too, are busy people.

Special projects: Another strategic tactic is to use special projects. At times, you may be able to coordinate a special project with some media outlet that benefits both of you. Keep in mind that any media outlet is a business and always needs a competitive edge. If you can provide this edge without alienating the other media in your community, you can reap great benefits.

The Santa Clara (Calif.) Unified School District identified a communication goal as "creating greater awareness of student writing success." It went to the local weekly newspaper and suggested that the schools provide a selection of short writing by students each week for a newspaper column. The paper accepted the idea and for years ran the column *Kids' Stuff*, which included limericks, poems, and other short items. It was positive news coverage, good for student morale, and sold newspapers. Everyone benefitted. The larger metropolitan daily wouldn't use something like this, so it wasn't a threat to that paper.

TV and radio interviews: Television and radio interviews require special strategies. Since they must be quickly understood by the listener and won't be repeated, communicators must take special care. Before doing any electronic interviews, you should be certain that you have time to

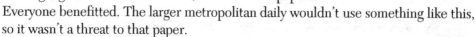

prepare, to think through what you want to say, to anticipate questions that might be asked, and to practice.

Thus, if a television reporter calls at 9:30 A.M. and says she will be at your school for an interview in 20 minutes, you could agree to the interview, but schedule it for noon. Also, ask the reporter about the interview to try to determine what her questions will be, what background she already has, and what direction the interview is likely to take.

To increase your chances of a successful interview, try these three preparation steps:

❖ develop message points;

❖ put them in clear, memorable language; and

❖ practice.

Message points are the thoughts you want to communicate during the interview. You should always have messages in mind for any interview — your communication goals — otherwise, why do the interview?

Always have messages in mind for any interview.

Don't have more than three message points for any interview, and write them down.

In a television interview, people will not be able to review what you say. They'll have to remember it the first time. That's why your message points need to be in memorable language, something that will stick in the listener's mind. For example, people still remember the memorable language from President Bush's presidential campaign: *Read my lips, no new taxes.*

Think about the questions the reporter is likely to ask and how you will work your message points into your answers. One key to success is the *bridging technique*. This means answering the question as quickly as possible, but then "bridging" to what you want to talk about — your message points.

How might this occur during an interview on declining test scores?

The scenario: Test scores have dropped two points at Premiere Elementary School and a television reporter wants an explanation from the principal. You want the interview to focus on what the school is doing to improve reading, not on the decline.

You establish two message points:

❖ the school is committed to improving reading scores, and

❖ parents must play an important role.

Your memorable language might be: *Reading's the priority at Premiere Elementary*, and *Reading's a family affair*.

Writing a News Release

News releases can be an effective way to communicate certain information from your school, such as awards and upcoming events. However, the media expect to receive releases written in a definite format.

Produce them in that format to increase chances of their use. Here are some things to think about:

❖ **Be as brief as possible.** Use short sentences, short paragraphs, and short words. Fewer, rather than more pages are desirable.

❖ **Write in a crisp, active style.** Forget educational jargon. Use one adjective instead of two, and keep your words moving. Use active (action), not passive verbs.

❖ **Put the most important information in the first parts of the release.** That way, if something needs to be cut, it can be cut from the bottom and the most important information will not be lost.

❖ *In your "lead," or first paragraph, deal with the five W's* (what, who, when, where, why) *and the H* (how), or as many of them as logically fit.

❖ *Double-space your release* and use only one side of the paper.

❖ *At the end of each page, except the last, center the word "- more -"* to indicate that the release continues. At the bottom of the last page, center three "###" to indicate that the release is finished.

❖ *Always have a contact name and telephone number at the top of the release* so the paper can ask questions or get more information.

 Sample News Release

FOR IMMEDIATE RELEASE   For further information contact : Your name
March 15, 2000   Your phone number

LOCAL STUDENT WINS STATE AWARD

Emily Howell, a sixth grade student at Premiere Elementary School has been named Virginia's Edison Science Award Winner for 2000, competing against more than 1,000 elementary school students from throughout the Commonwealth.

Howell earned the award last weekend during the annual State Edison Science Championships in Richmond. More than 200 elementary students competed, and awards were presented by Governor Doug Gilmore.

"Emily capped an outstanding elementary school experience in science and math and made our entire staff and fellow students proud of her accomplishments," said Principal Rich Bagin. "She has been involved in our science club and mathletes program since third grade," Bagin added.

This is the second time in five years Premiere Elementary has had the top Edison Award Winner in the Commonwealth. Steve Bosnick won the same award in 1995.

- more -

Another good way to communicate with the news media that doesn't require as much writing as a news release is a news "tipsheet."

Here you write a short, crisp paragraph describing a possible news story. Include a contact's name and phone number and send that to the reporter or assignment editor.

One tipsheet could include several ideas. For instance, a school could send a tipsheet at the start of the year describing new instructional programs for the coming school year.

Creating a Pipeline for News

Often staff do not inform you of the activities that need to be included in news releases, newsletters, bulletins, and websites. One way for them to give you this information is to develop a fact sheet to serve as news pipeline.

A sample fact sheet follows and it is also in your tool kit ready for duplication.

❖ *Sample Fact Sheet*

Use this form to describe interesting class or school events, programs, or projects and news involving your staff members and students. For best results, give the information to the principal's office in advance (two weeks is best).

Fill in the appropriate items. Attach additional information, if necessary.

Teacher _____ Date _____

1. **Who** List people involved, titles, grades, etc.

   _____
   _____
   _____
   _____

2. **What** Describe award, event, program, project, etc.

   _____
   _____
   _____
   _____

3. **Where** Place

   _____
   _____
   _____
   _____

4. **When**   Dates and times

       _____

       _____

       _____

5. **Why or how** Reason for award, event, project, etc.

       _____

       _____

       _____

6. **Points of special interest**

       _____

       _____

       _____

       _____

Please forward this form to the principal's office at least two weeks before the planned event.

Communicating in a Crisis

None of today's school leaders went into education prepared for the myriad crises that now occur in schools. However, they've all learned that it is essential to anticipate and prepare for crises. It's almost certain that you will experience a crisis at some point in your career, and it seems, crises are becoming much worse. While a broken boiler used to be defined as a crisis, schools now face hostage situations, shootings, intruders, suicides, and other instances unheard of even 15 years ago.

*I*t's almost certain that you will experience a crisis at some point in your career.

Although you can't avoid all crises, you can plan how to anticipate and manage them. Planning is essential because of the impact that a crisis can have on people and on the long-term reputation of your school. There's no more difficult time to lead, and it's a time when years of quality performance can be destroyed in 24 hours.

While crises are diverse and must be managed from your local perspective, certain common recommendations apply:

❖ **All schools — and school districts — should have crisis plans**, and you should be very familiar with yours. If your school doesn't have a crisis plan, create it now.

You may want to contact a respected colleague or two to see if they have a crisis plan that they would be willing to share. NSPRA has prepared *The Complete Crisis Communication Management Manual for Schools*, which contains considerable advice and samples.

However, be sure that your plan reflects your needs and situation. While you may want to review other plans, you should develop one that is specific for your school and community.

❖ **Be prepared**. Know your plan and make sure that other key people on your staff are aware of it and understand how to implement it. It's wise to periodically practice and update your plan; it's an investment that could save your reputation and your school's reputation.

❖ **Never speak before you know what you want to say.** This sounds obvious, but many educators have added fuel to a crisis fire by announcing inaccurate information. You need a mechanism in place to gather data quickly. And, while it's important to provide information quickly, it's more important to ensure that information is accurate.

❖ **Know which of your publics need to know which information first.** If a crisis affects students — ranging from head lice to a hostage situation — parents will want instant information. If you can provide that, you will increase your reputation as a caring, responsive school. If not, some people may conclude that things are out of control and the school is without direction.

❖ **Develop sample materials that you can easily adapt when the crisis hits.** For example, a frequently used communication vehicle in a crisis situation is the *Dear Parent* letter. This is typically sent home the first day to inform parents of the situation and to ensure that all are receiving the same information.

However, developing a letter when you are trying to manage a crisis is difficult. It makes more sense to draft a sample letter now and have a trusted staff member fill in the blanks when the situation occurs. Also, be sure to have a set of mailing labels ready to go.

❖ **Be prepared for the news media.** Even though you have never been covered by the local news media, they will arrive when a crisis occurs. If the crisis is major, you may be covered by wire services, network television, and even "sensationalistic" TV shows.

When you need to release information quickly during a crisis, you need the media's help.

Consider the following issues ahead of time:

❖ **Who will be the spokesperson?** Designate one person as the primary spokesperson. You might name the school system public relations professional, if there is one, or a trusted individual on the school staff.

Sometimes the best spokesperson is the principal or superintendent. When a major statement is to be released, parents, and community leaders expect to hear it from the "chief executive officer." However, that person is also responsible for managing the situation and will not have time to announce nitty-gritty details every other hour.

You need to determine who will speak on what issues, balancing time requirements with reputational concerns. However, keep in mind that the more people who speak, the more likely that mixed messages will be communicated.

❖ **What is the camera policy?** Television cameras in the school could be very disruptive at a time when you least need disruption. Determine in advance how you hope to handle cameras, but also consider the needs of the news media.

It's a good idea to have a Board-adopted policy about cameras in schools during a crisis. Remember, however, that TV crews can set up on the sidewalk and interview students and staff as they leave school if you are not responsive to their needs. The best approach may be to establish a policy that bars cameras from school buildings during a crisis, discuss that policy with TV assignment editors so they will understand your rationale before the crisis hits, and then establish other ways to meet the news media's needs.

Determine in advance how you hope to handle cameras.

❖ **Build a positive relationship with the news media by providing information in an organized manner.** Have a procedure in place to collect relevant data and to quickly confirm its accuracy. If many reporters cover the situation, it's wise to make your initial release of information at a news conference so that all news media get the same information at the same time.

Devoting 30 minutes to a news conference is a much better use of time than spending 15 minutes individually on the phone with 10 reporters. If the crisis lasts several days, schedule news conferences each day. While information is being collected and verified, someone else should alert the news media about when and where the news conference will be held.

❖ **Develop a list of newspapers and television and radio stations in advance,** including the key contact people, phone numbers, and deadlines. Knowing deadlines will help you schedule news conferences (and being ignorant of reporters' deadlines will only cause difficulties for both you and them).

Try to get telephone numbers directly into radio and TV news rooms. If the boiler bursts at 3 A.M. and you need to alert students not to come to school, a radio station's closed switchboard won't do you much good.

NSPRA's *The Complete Crisis Communication Management Manual for Schools* provides the following perspective of news media needs during a crisis:

The Media Perspective

❖ In crisis situations, an adversarial relationship may occur between the district and a news outlet, especially if good relationships have not existed in the past.

❖ The media consider the district spokesperson as someone who will paint the best possible picture of all elements of a disaster or crisis.

❖ The media may want to blame someone or some thing — a staff member's error, some structural defect or lack of maintenance in the building, etc.

❖ The media do not consider the spokesperson as the only source of information. They will try to interview other people involved, such as the principal, staff, students, parents, counselors, etc. They are seeking the full story and a variety of perspectives.

> *The media do not consider the spokesperson as the only source of information.*

❖ In some crisis situations, you may want to designate a "press area." Indoors, this should include telephones, tables, chairs, etc.

❖ The news media do not have a right to interfere with the educational process. They do not have a right to enter a school building when school is in session.

❖ It is a judgment call whether the news media should be allowed on a school campus or not. In the case of a student demonstration — no, don't allow them on campus. In the case of a hostage situation, perhaps. The news media may use any public property, such as sidewalks or a park, and may interview staff, students or parents there.

❖ If it is appropriate, arrange for several students to meet with reporters. While you might be inclined to use student leaders who are "comfortable" in sharing the general feelings of the student body, it would be more credible to select volunteers who are willing to meet with the reporters. Have a school administrator present during interviews with students.

❖ The news media's role is to publicize information that people want. They see their role as informing parents and others in the community. For instance, in an incident with an assault rifle on a school campus, the first thing parents want to know is, "*Is my kid all right?*" Accurate reporting on how many children have been injured and what is happening to the children who have not been injured is important. The news media can best get that information quickly to parents, rather than having all of them descend on the school.

❖ If the district does not respond to reporters' questions in a timely manner, the media may assume that the district is trying to hide something or is indifferent. Being unresponsive to the news media is the quickest way to ensure an adversarial relationship. If a reporter believes that the district is lying, they will assume that the district is trying to lie to the public as well.

> **B**eing unresponsive is the quickest way to ensure an adversarial relationship.

Some Essential Points

❖ If something bad happens in a school or a district, the news media is almost sure to find out about it — through a telephone call from a student, staff member, or parent, or by listening to the police radio.

❖ Frequently an adversarial relationship exists between the news media and school administrators because reporters believe that administrators will only talk about "good" things and will try to hide "bad" things — which is generally true.

❖ Be prepared to come under news media scrutiny. As a public official, you must be prepared for media coverage, not all of which will be flattering about your school or yourself.

❖ Understand that different media have different agendas and compete among themselves. The nature of that competition will play a part in how they conduct themselves at a news gathering.

❖ The news media has a right to all student "directory information," within the meaning of the term in federal law, unless the parent has requested that this information be withheld. This includes a picture in a school yearbook. Learn what you have a right to withhold and what you must release. Don't refuse to release something or stall its release if you'll be required to release it in the long run; that only strengthens adversarial relationships with the media. Call the district's public information office if you're unsure about your state's public information law.

❖ Avoid educational jargon. If you must use it, explain what it means.

❖ Don't slight the broadcast media in favor of print or vice versa, although there will be times when one is more valuable to you than the other.

❖ Don't stereotype reporters — unless you welcome the same treatment of educators. Judge reporters as individuals according to the accuracy and fairness of their stories.

❖ If a reporter has done what you consider a good job, make it a point to let them know that.

❖ Remember your very important audiences. While the news media will disseminate the news throughout the community, some key audiences should hear directly from you. For example, if a shooting has occurred on campus, you don't want the superintendent or board members to learn about it by listening to the radio.

Among the most important audiences are central office staff, school staff, parents, students, and your Key Communicator network. Have a procedure to reach all of them.

❖ Make sure that you have a list of key phone numbers, and carry it with you all the time. This might include the police and fire departments, superintendent, key members of your administrative team, custodian and civil defense office. Home phone numbers would be essential during a crisis.

Frequently, your success during a crisis will be determined during the first 30 minutes of the crisis. The following advice comes from NSPRA's *The Complete Crisis Communication Management Manual for Schools.*

What is done in the first 30 minutes is crucial to determining people's perceptions.

The First 30 Minutes

What is done in the first 30 minutes of a crisis is crucial in determining people's perceptions of the crisis and how it was handled.

❖ *Have the appropriate person handle the situation*. The administrator (the principal or superintendent) should take charge of the situation, implementing the crisis plan.

❖ *Understand the circumstances*; define the problems.

❖ *Consider the options*; act decisively to ensure the health and safety of students and staff and protection of district property.

❖ *Communicate with staff*; keep the news media informed.

❖ *Update students periodically* in their classrooms. Avoid having large group meetings.

❖ *Inform parents by a letter*, sent home with students at the end of the day, explaining what occurred and what has been done about it.

❖ *The community will be interested, too.* To allay fears and demonstrate competence in handling the situation, get accurate information out through the news media and key communicators, such as the PTA president and executive board.

❖ *Implement a Crisis Assessment and Information Sheet*, similar to the sheet on the next page.

The First 30 Minutes:
Crisis Assessment and Information Sheet

Briefly describe the crisis _____
_____
_____

Actions completed _____
_____
_____

Who now knows of crisis _____   _____
_____   _____
_____   _____
_____   _____
_____   _____

Assessment of damage or harm to people:

Number of people involved _____

How many unaccounted for _____

Injuries (Briefly describe seriousness.)_____
_____
_____

Evacuation needed?   ❏   Yes

❏   No

Assessment of damage to buildings:

Briefly describe damage: _____

_____

_____

Further damage potential _____

_____

Other facilities at risk _____

_____

What do you project will happen in the next two hours? _____

_____

_____

_____

Dealing with the news media:

Are media on site? ❑ Yes Who? _____

❑ How many? _____

No

Check the resources you need:

❑ Crisis manager ❑ Construction ❑ Clerical
❑ Social/Guidance counselor ❑ Communications ❑ Insurance/Claims
❑ Medical ❑ Media relations ❑ Legal
❑ Safety ❑ Transportation ❑ Others
❑ Food service

Your name _____

Time _____ Phone number _____

FAX number _____

FAX the completed form to your superintendent's office as soon as possible to receive the appropriate assistance.

Building-level Crises: Principal's Checklist

Principals who have experienced and survived a crisis understand the importance of planning, maintaining and updating checklists, and completing forms quickly and accurately to ensure an accurate record of events.

This information is from NSPRA's *The Complete Crisis Communication Management Manual for Schools* and gives you practical advice developed over years of experience.

❖ Each August, list those people who may be named acting principal for your building when you're absent; post it in the administrative office. Give each staff member a copy to post with their classroom checklists.

> **L**ist those people who may be named acting principal when you're absent.

❖ Each August, with the acting principal designees and custodians, review all utility turn-off points; check the ability of each person to operate these safely. Include gas, oil, water, electricity, and boilers.

❖ Develop a telephone tree for your building staff. Give each person on the list 5 to 8 people to call in case of an emergency.

❖ Have first-aid equipment and instructions in designated areas.

❖ Every year, review the teacher crisis checklist with your staff and be certain that teachers have this checklist available at their desks.

❖ Also every year, review the custodian crisis checklist with your staff and check to see that it is posted in the custodial area.

❖ In time of crisis, you must be easily identified. Have an orange armband available for wearing in crisis situations.

❖ During a crisis, confirm that a roll count of students and staff is taken and sent to the office or command post.

❖ If a student is released to an individual other than a parent, ask to see identification and get that person to write down:

— the student's name,
— the name of the person picking the student up,
— the time, and
— the destination.

During a crisis, confirm that a roll count of students and staff is taken.

Who's In Charge When the Principal Is Away?

As the principal of a school, you're responsible for the students and staff in your building. Whenever you're absent from the school, you must designate a certified staff member to be the acting principal and to make decisions during any crisis that may occur.

Always post a list of people who may be named acting principal when you are absent, and before leaving, make sure you determine who the acting principal is for a specific period of time.

All building staff need to know who the acting principal is every time you're absent. Post this list in the office, in the staff lounge, and in other appropriate locations.

These people are designated to act as principal in my absence:	Their home phone numbers:

Give anyone designated as acting principals a copy of the *Crisis Communication/ Management Manual* or make sure they know where it is. They need to become familiar with the book and know how to use it.

❖ ### A Gun at School: What Would You Do?

Just after lunch, your second-grade teacher comes into your office with a seven-year-old student and the loaded .22-caliber handgun that he pulled out of his backpack to show to a classmate.

Now what?

That's exactly what happened — the first time in his 31 years — to principal Bob Ziegler at New Hope Elementary, a middle-income, 520-student, suburban school about eight miles outside of Minneapolis. Ziegler and his staff handled it smoothly, without incident, because they were prepared and used common sense and PR skills.

They were under a lot of pressure. "We were the lead story on all four TV channels, in all the papers, and it was broadcast on Minnesota Public Radio and on the AP wire all over the country," said Ziegler. "Satellite trucks were broadcasting live from our parking lot. Reporters even drove 20 miles to my home that evening for a 10 o'clock news piece."

Have a Policy

No matter how much we hear or read about weapons in school, most of us consider them relatively rare in the lower grades. But are they?

"A recent report from an eastern state showed that firearm possessions at school begin in fifth or sixth grades and peak by eighth or ninth," says Ron Stephens, director of the National School Safety Center. "These statistics are consistent with school crime data maintained by school systems across the country."

Whether this peak means younger students have more access to weapons or older kids simply don't get caught, K-8 principals must be prepared as firearms continue to come to school.

Stephens cautioned that each weapon situation is unique and needs to be evaluated and approached in an individual way. "Knowing the children is the first step," he said. He recommends that safety and crisis procedures be in place and that every staff member be trained and regularly reminded of the process.

New Hope's Plan

Bob Ziegler's district was prepared. A new comprehensive crisis policy — developed with parents, attorneys, and principals — was mailed to every family last September. Each student was then responsible for getting parents' signatures on a special card to prove that they had read and understood the policy. "Having a policy was extremely important," says Ziegler. "Since everyone was familiar with it, I knew what I had to do and *they* knew it, too."

The first 10 minutes were critical. First, Ziegler called the boy's father, because it was the dad's weapon. Next, he informed his superintendent, and then the police. "The father was very apologetic and had no idea his son knew about the gun," Ziegler explained. Nevertheless, following the district policy, Ziegler immediately suspended the student.

The police arrived and took a report and the gun. The mother came to take her son home. Two central office employees rushed to New Hope and helped Ziegler write and reproduce a well-worded, factual announcement for parents.

"I got on the PA to announce that the buses would be about five minutes late because there was an important announcement that each child must take home," he says, not mentioning what had happened.

Keep Staff Informed

When the buses pulled out, a faculty meeting was held to give staff a full explanation. Ziegler made it clear, also, that he was the only spokesperson. "Handling this was a team effort," says Ziegler, "and the staff was wonderful. But I cautioned them not to comment, to simply answer questions with the facts, and to refer any media questions to me."

Of course, the moment the notice hit home, the media got wind of the incident and their siege began. Ziegler again handled it calmly, always protecting the child's privacy and sticking to the facts. It did help, he feels, that he already had a positive relationship with many reporters. "Except for a few minor things, the news coverage was very accurate," he says.

Here's what Ziegler recommends to principals who find themselves in a similar situation:

❖ **Have a crisis plan and stick to it.** Ziegler says that it was difficult to suspend a seven-year-old, but since all the parents had been informed, they understood.

❖ If you don't have a school public information officer to advise you and help write a notice to parents, **get some help** from another principal.

❖ **Have *one* spokesperson**.

❖ **Stick to the facts.** Don't comment or speculate, especially on the air. Just stop talking. Reporters will fill the dead air.

❖ **Respect privacy.** Ziegler *never* named children or teachers or mentioned home locations.

The Morning After

In the morning — after shooing reporters away from parents who were dropping children off—Ziegler met the child's father and arranged for homebound instruction. (At that mandatory hearing the child received a five-day expulsion and then transferred to a new school. State law requires that parents reveal — to the new principal — the reason for expulsion.)

Next, Ziegler met with his staff, reinforcing the *one* spokesperson message, and to bring them up to date. One attention-starved child, for instance, had gone on television with a lot of wrong information about the incident. Ziegler later challenged the child, his parent, and the TV station.

Making It a Lesson

"The second morning I talked with the children and turned this unfortunate event into a learning situation," he said. "I told them not to be afraid, that we had everything under control. I asked them to go home and talk with their parents about placing guns in a locked location at home, and to immediately tell adults at school or home — or anywhere — if they saw a dangerous situation."

The third morning, Ziegler got to school early with donuts and coffee for his staff. They put this chapter behind them. And Ziegler has turned down any media requests for follow-up information. "It's over and we're back to normal," he said. That's a good ending and good PR.

June Million
Public Information Director
NAESP

From the February 1996 issue of *Communicator*

Communicating Through Newsletters

Communicating through publications is still one of the best vehicles you have to regularly deliver information to parents. Most principals today either have a school or principal's newsletter going to parents and other groups. Often it is funded by a parent group and contains key messages on upcoming parent group activities.

In addition, some principals also encourage individual teachers to produce classroom newsletters or grade-level newsletters which focus more on what learning is taken place in classrooms. Remember, the more focused and relevant you can make a newsletter, the better read it will be.

Some principals also include a question-and-answer format in their newsletters. If you receive a number of inquires about a certain issue in your school, it may be good to address that issue in your newsletter.

Today's technology also allows you to receive extra mileage from your newsletter efforts. Since you spent the time to put a newsletter together at least once a month, save it, and place the newsletter on your school's website.

> *The more focused and relevant you make a newsletter, the better read it will be.*

Doing so gives you two separate vehicles to inform your parents and the website can keep the back issues on file for later use. Putting the newsletter online can also serve as a safety net for those parents who say they never received a copy.

The following advice should help you either improve your current newsletter or start one:

Why a Newsletter?

By contrast with most printed material, a school newsletter is read when it reaches home. Studies have shown that parents rate the school newsletter as their second-most important source of information about the schools. The most important is what their children say about school.

If it is a good vehicle, your newsletter is an important instrument to:

❖ Build support for the school program;

❖ Keep accurate information before the people who "own the schools;"

❖ Make people aware of programs, events, and challenges of the school;

❖ Increase community involvement, participation, and attendance at school functions;

❖ Make citizens aware of the importance of public education in relation to the quality of life in the community;

❖ Contribute to the improvement of the educational program; and

❖ Assist parents in helping their children learn.

In addition, your newsletter reflects something about you as principal:

Your newsletter reflects something about you as a principal.

❖ It's the only regular contact you have with most of your parents — and, therefore, a prime way that you convey what kind of person you are and what kind of school you run.

❖ It's a letter, which implies that you value this contact with parents and are willing to extend yourself to gain their interest.

❖ It contains news, which implies you believe they're entitled to know what's going on, and you enjoy sharing things with them.

What About a Name?

❖ Keep it simple.

❖ Be sure people can identify with it.

❖ Don't keep changing it.

❖ Establish a visual image.

Who Should Receive It?

❖ The school family:

— Professional personnel

— Support personnel

— Student teachers

— Regular volunteers

— Substitute teachers

— Parents of *all* students in your school

— Board of Education members

— Central office staff members, including the communication professional

— Principals, secretaries, guidance counselors, team leaders, parent group leaders of the schools you feed in to

❖ The school community:

— Nonparents/Key communicator network

— Local neighbors to your school

— Businesspeople

— Ministers

— Area chamber of commerce

— Area weekly newspapers

— Presidents of major area civic and service clubs in your attendance area

When and How Should the Newsletter Be Distributed?

❖ Brief newsletters are better than long ones. The more frequently the newsletter is published, the fresher the news is. The "news package" is smaller and the newsletter has a better chance of being read. A general rule is to publish at least monthly, if not more frequently.

❖ Establish a regular schedule for the newsletter. It's better to publish frequently with fewer pages than it is to publish infrequently with many pages. Hit-and-miss publications generate disregard for the contents.

❖ Send the newsletter with the youngest student in each family. Sending a publication home with students probably won't be successful after the students are in the sixth grade. Mail it in these cases with bulk mailing permit.

❖ Periodically check on the efficiency of the distribution system. Consider calling parents to see if they received the last newsletter and if they have any questions.

❖ Encourage all school employees to regularly take copies of their newsletters to their barber and beauty shops and doctors' and dentists' offices. And don't forget the waiting areas of the Jiffy Lube and other quick auto repair vendors.

How to Gather News and Get Ideas

❖ Create opportunities for all staff members to share in the content of the publication. An effective tool for doing this is to distribute a news pipeline sheet contained in this guide to staff members (*See a sample in this section of workbook*).

❖ Work with an advisory committee of interested parents to help determine the kind of content of greatest interest to the most people.

❖ At PTA and citizens' meetings, keep your ears tuned for concerns and inquiries.

❖ If your school has a suggestion box, find out what's being recommended.

❖ Keep track of the kind of telephone calls that come into the school office for a three- or four-day period. Analyze the kinds of questions parents have, and then make certain that future issues deal with those concerns.

❖ Identify the person or persons responsible for preparing each issue of the newsletter. This information can be placed in a masthead box at the end of the newsletter, together with the address of the school and how the person may be contacted.

What to Write About

While this may seem to be a problem at first, once you get started the question will be what to leave out. With limited space and stories in every classroom waiting to be told, it boils down to a matter of selecting the most interesting and informative.

One good technique is to use the "who cares" formula:

❖ The more who care, the more significant the news is.

❖ The more significant news should come first.

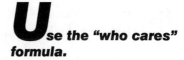

In general, these elements affect news:
❖ Timeliness
❖ Proximity
❖ Prominence
❖ Consequence (importance)
❖ Human interest
❖ Conflict

As idea starters, you might consider some of these topics:

❖ News about school activities, especially classroom activities

❖ School safety (pickup and delivery of students to school, etc.)

❖ Discussion of real or potential school problems and what's being done to cope with them. (Parents are usually relieved to know the school is aware of the situation and working on it.)

❖ How staff development programs on early release days better prepare teachers and specific activities in which they participate.

❖ Opportunities for parents to help at school, such as a volunteer program, principals advisory committee, school crossing guards for kindergarten students released at noon, room mothers, etc.

❖ Personality sketch of teacher, secretary, food service employee, custodian, principal, assistant principal, counselor, school crossing guard

❖ Awards, recognition, advanced degrees earned by teachers and other school employees

❖ Awards, special recognition, unusual leadership of students — perhaps even a "Student of the Month" for outstanding citizenship

❖ Brief, significant message from principal

❖ Presentation of the facts about rumors which are circulating, such as the closing of a school

❖ Calendar of coming events for your particular school

❖ Which staff member to contact for various areas of responsibility

❖ What's being done to challenge outstanding students

❖ How your instructional program is meeting the individual needs of students

❖ Brief summaries of important parent group business

❖ Dates and deadlines of importance

❖ Condensation of speeches made by staff members or by community residents to classes

Add reminder news items to any given issue. For example: school hours, noon hour procedures, or PTA meetings, etc.

It doesn't hurt to repeat important information because it may have been overlooked, forgotten, or never have reached home last issue. For the sake of those who did read and remember, re-write the news and try to freshen it with late developments.

 Newsletter Evaluation Form

Our aim in publishing *The Premiere News* is to provide readers with timely, accurate information that meets their communication needs. We want to make sure that we're providing what you want, and the only way we can be sure is by asking you.

So, please take a few moments to fill out this short questionnaire. Return it to Rich Bagin, principal, Premiere Elementary School, Raybury Road, Arlington, VA 22091. Thanks!

1. How many times did you receive *The Premiere News* this year?

    ❏ 3 times

    ❏ 5 times

    ❏ 9 times

    ❏ not at all

2. How would you describe the writing style in *The Premiere News*?

    ❏ readable

    ❏ too difficult to understand

    ❏ just right

3. How would you describe the appearance of *The Premiere News*?

    ❏ attractive

    ❏ boring

    ❏ functional

4. What part of *The Premiere News* do you like the most?

    _____

    _____

5. What part of *The Premiere News* do you like the least?

    _____

    _____

6. What topics would you like to see covered next year?

    _____

    _____

7. What else would you like to tell us?

    _____

    _____

Community Outlets for School Information

Often, school leaders overlook obvious community outlets where they can place their yearbooks, school newspapers, school newsletters, and updates of accomplishments.

1. First, look at your immediate attendance areas for community spots, such as municipal buildings, waiting rooms of doctors' offices, quick-lube auto shops, libraries, and senior citizen centers.

2. Also, make sure that copies are sent out and displayed in your feeder schools and nursery schools in your system.

3. Next, find out where many of your parents work; see if extra copies can be sent to their workplace. As more and more outlets are used, your entire community will learn a great deal more about your school.

Outlets in our attendance area

_____   _____
_____   _____
_____   _____

Feeder schools and nursery schools

_____   _____
_____   _____
_____   _____

Parent workplaces

_____   _____
_____   _____
_____   _____

Principals in the Public

5 Technology

Technology will enhance your public engagement efforts

Websites, homework hotlines, classroom websites and electronic bulletin boards, group email transmissions, individual email, broadcast fax transmissions, fax-on-demand, voicemail, messaging centers, videos, PowerPoint presentations, cell phones, low-wattage radio… what's a busy principal to do?

The ever-increasing role of technology in today's communication efforts will enhance your public engagement efforts. But technology falls into the category of being a "double-edged sword" because it can be very effective, and yet it can require constant attention for changing messages on a regular basis.

Be cautious in the type of electronic communication you choose because you need to be assured that regular updates can be completed before embarking on a new technology venture.

Be cautious in the type of electronic communication you choose.

This is another area where the principal cannot do it all alone.

An increasing number of technology/publishing companies have also begun working with individual schools and school districts to provide the templates for websites and the software for easy electronic communication between homes and the school. Many of these offerings are free to schools and are worth investigating.

If you attend just about any state or national principal's convention, you'll surely be contacted by yet another vendor who is hoping to sell you the latest homework hotline, homepage software, and voice-mail system.

How do you know where to start? Let's first look at how schools around the country are now using technology:

Message Centers

Many schools offer a telephone number as the information line on school activities. Either it's the standard answering machine or a service purchased by a telecommunications vendor that gives out information about upcoming events, school closings, and other pertinent information. Some schools include the daily menu on their information line as well.

With a message center, you must:

❖ update messages frequently,

❖ maintain security pass codes for changing the message, and

❖ gather correct messages to include on the service.

You also have to print the phone number on all school materials so that parents and students know that it is readily available.

If you consider using a message center, make sure that a system is in place for someone to quickly fill in for the person in charge of the center if he or she is sick, has a death in the family, or has another type of crisis and cannot handle the task.

Also, look into services or products which allow you to change the message from your home or cellular phone.

Be sure to have a number of lines available that can pick up from the one phone number because callers will see the system as a waste of time and money if they always receive a busy signal. Telecommunications vendors will gladly help you with this "opportunity." You may also want to ask them about ways to track the number of calls you receive.

Primarily, these systems are one-way — they just give out information. Some systems do allow for messages to be taken, but that's another consideration covered in the voice-mail section.

Voice-Mail Boxes

Talk to 10 people and you'll probably find five who like voice mail and five who hate it. We can all relate to listening to the now ubiquitous "Voice-Mail Lady" saying,

> "Thank you for calling Premiere Elementary School. If you know the number of the person you wish to reach, dial that number now; if not dial *xix* for our directory… and if you still need help…."

So why consider it? Because voice-mail can work and be most impressive to parents and others who want to leave messages with key staff members. And it doesn't even have to be that expensive. (*See "Technology Opens Communication for Budget-minded Principal" about the principal who rigged his own voice-mail system using a less-than-powerful computer.*)

Some schools now give a voice-mail box to every teacher. Just what the teacher does with it is up to the planning team recommendations.

❖ Some teachers use it only as an answering device to take messages from parents and others.

❖ Others use it to give periodic information (about upcoming tests, project due dates, and topics being covered in class).

❖ Still others use it to give daily homework assignments.

The range of messages also dictates the amount of work it takes to maintain the system. From a public relations and customer service standpoint, it is imperative that the message sounds friendly, professional, and as enthusiastic as possible. Otherwise, your school reputation can easily be torn down by a number of teachers whose messages are less than desired.

But the most important aspect of a voice-mail system is the teacher, counselor, secretary, and principal's response time to the call in the voice-mail box. Have your planning committee agree on the acceptable response time, tell parents and others what that response time is, and adhere to it. Otherwise, your voice-mail system will do you more harm than good.

> *The most important aspect of a voice-mail system is response time.*

Some teachers have lost their jobs in school districts because they refused to answer voice-mail in a reasonable timeframe. They said that such duties were not part of their job. The school district thought differently.

As technology advances, some voice-mail systems also allow you to record one message that can be sent to pre-selected groups. Examples could be a message to all staff, a reminder to the executive committee of the PTA, a message to all your third grade parents, etc. The cost of these sophisticated systems continue to come down, but you may want to investigate the feasibility of using group voice mail in your school.

 Technology Opens Communication for Budget-Minded Principal

When elementary school principal Gregory Kuhns went shopping for a voice-mail system, he didn't let the $10,000 price tag stop him.

Kuhns sat down, rolled up his sleeves, and got busy learning about computers and for about $500, he was able to install a 24-hour hotline for parents, staff, and students.

The voice messaging system at Watson Elementary School in Fairmont, W. Va., provides information about the school's policies, procedures, coming events, and daily menus.

Teachers use the system to remind students of homework assignments and tests and to tell parents good news about their child. The PTA notifies members of committee meetings, and the district's emergency phone numbers are programmed into the system. It even has a built-in fax machine. "We've used it about every way possible," says Kuhns.

Parents who use the system give it high ratings in school surveys. About 40% of the parents in the 400-student school take advantage of it.

Those teachers who use it report more students remember to bring in materials after they're received reminders on voice mail, and test scores appear to have risen.

The principal's job has benefitted too, says Kuhns. For example, school lunch menus are posted on the phone system, reducing time spent on answering phone calls. He also programmed the system to call teachers when school is canceled because of snow.

This fall, Kuhns is in a unique position to start over in introducing a voice messaging system to a new elementary school. As incoming principal of St. James Elementary School in Myrtle Beach, S.C., he's dedicated to expanding voice mail to include business and the community to gain support of schools.

"I'm just trying to open that line of communication a little wider. And being a new principal, I want them to know right away," he said.

The second time around, Kuhns will also try to boost usage by improving staff training and evaluation of the system.

He found out the first time that some teachers had a hard time buying into the system. "At first, they didn't want to take the time and they were leery of computers," Kuhns said. "They have to be trained and comfortable or they won't use it."

A voice mail system really needs to be personal and friendly to work best, Kuhns believes. He designed it so his voice is heard, not a digitized computer voice. And a voice mailbox number can be punched in at any time during the introduction, rather than waiting for a long list of options.

Although his new school in South Carolina has more money available for technology, Kuhns plans on spending about $200 to install a new system himself. At his former school, the PTA and a local bank chipped in to pay for the $35 average monthly phone bill for the system.

The system also needs to be fun. Kuhns initiated a treasure hunt, disclosing one clue on the voice mail system every week for five weeks. He also used the system to provide science experiments for a semester to get students used to calling in.

— from *It Starts on the Frontline*, NSPRA.

Keep in mind that all callers may not be reasonable. Some parents will call every day just to check that everything is okay. Others will call to argue about the latest grade given on an essay test. You must cover such inconsiderate abuses of voice-mail systems in parent handbooks, principals' newsletters, parent meetings, etc. If everyone agrees on the ground rules going in and abides by them and the agreed-upon consequences, a voice-mail box system can boost your school communication program. After you thoroughly explain the new voice-mail system to your staff, provide training, and list the expectations and guidelines, you're ready to announce it to parents.

 Staff Involvement Is Key

Leading principals put together a team of staff members and an advisory council of students and parents to tackle some of the nitty-gritty "opportunities" presented by the use of telecommunications in their school's PR effort. Staff involvement, training, participation, and "buy-in" are key to making your effort a success.

This team approach leads to guidelines that will drive the use of your system.

❖ Just how quickly are teachers expected to react to voice-mail or e-mail?

❖ How often are sections of your homepage updated?

❖ What is an unreasonable number of messages left by a parent?

❖ *And the big accountability questions:* What happens when these guidelines are ignored by staff or parents or students?

These questions need answers and guidelines need to be agreed to before you announce your program to your parents and students. Not to do so can only lead to problems that will take more than technology to fix.

Consider these tasks when you introduce the new voice-mail system to parents:

❖ List numbers in the parent handbook, along with guidelines and voice-mail etiquette principles.

❖ Send home a brochure listing much of the information in the handbook, with examples of the types of questions that parents may frequently ask.

All About Voice-mail

❖ Hold a special PTA meeting about the system and demonstrate to parents how to use the system.

❖ Place a feature story in the local paper explaining the new initiatives with testimonials from your staff and parents.

❖ Convene a three-month review meeting with the PTA on the success of the program and recommendations for improvement.

A major plus of a voice-mail box system or the message information center is that most homes today have access to a phone. You can reach most parents and homes through these systems.

Internet Communication

More and more schools are entering into the Internet Age with their schools now offering a homepage. Students and parents can access the page at any time from home, the office, or the local library. A homepage can give you the opportunity to post pertinent information that meets the needs of your parents and students, and it can also give you e-mail access to parents and others.

You first have to decide just what content items you want your homepage to carry. Then project how that content will be maintained. Unless you have a great amount of staff time to assist you on this project, we urge you to ease into your homepage efforts.

Let's look at some of the information we now see being carried on homepages:

❖ **Short introduction** on how to get the most out of the homepage, including shortcut commands that can help your readers get the information that they really want

❖ **Event information** on upcoming meetings, special programs, days off and, yes, even lunch menus

❖ **Directory** of phone numbers and e-mail numbers for teaching and counseling staff, as well as the secretaries and all administrative personnel

❖ **Pertinent information** from student and parent handbooks — policies and procedures on attendance, discipline, gym procedures, co-curricular activities, etc.

❖ **Synopsis of course content** for every subject and grade level

❖ **Latest issue of the school newspaper** and school or principal's newsletter

❖ **Attendance areas and bus schedules** for your school

❖ Listing of **honor roll students**

❖ **Test score results** for the past five years

❖ **Profiles of students**-of-the-week or -of-the-month for each grade level in your school

❖ Always carry **emergency bulletins** in the opening menu that will supersede any other information. Examples include a heating room boiler breakdown, a bank robbery across the street from your school and the suspect is thought to be hiding in your attendance area, etc.

❖ **Reports on controversial news coverage** that tell your side of the story — the fact that the drug bust in your school's parking lot involved only kids from a nearby private school

❖ **Hot links** to other services going deeper into instructional areas so parents and others can actually tap into some of the resources now used by your school

❖ **PTA events** and programs

❖ **Parenting assistance** to help parents better tutor their students

❖ **Fund-raising events**, such as read-a-thons, grocery receipts for computers, wrapping paper, and canned goods drives

The list goes on and on. You need to work with a group of parents, staff members, and students to determine where you should begin. Then develop a responsibility plan to deliver and update that information.

We see a division of responsibility for many menu items in homepages. Often students are recruited to help maintain a section of the homepage, and staff members are given sections so that the burden doesn't fall on just one person.

You also need to make sure that access to making changes on your homepage is secure. You don't want a local hacker to break into your system and announce that school will be closed or that Thursday's menu will consist of mystery meat or something much worse. Passwords cut the chances of these miscues happening, but the system must be kept secure.

A number of new homepage software programs are now available. Contact the technology expert in your central office to see what your district may have available. Also check out the following two recently developed and free resources for telecommunications assistance. Some of these companies provide customized features so that teachers can send group mail to their parents, develop electronic bulletin boards for parents, and also provide information about your school as well as national education news that is relevant to parents. One even offers translation services for parents.

Two companies offering a range of services are:

❖ The Family Education Network at familyeducation.com, and

❖ Copernicus at edgate.com.

In addition, here's what NAESP's *Communicator* had to say about principals and their webpages:

 The Buck Stops at the Principal's Office

You only get one chance to make a first impression. So, just as the school's front door or your secretary's phone manners can make or break your reputation, your school web site can do the same. What does the world see when it visits your site? Fluff or useful content? A menu that includes general information, handbook rules, and staff backgrounds, plus special programs, lunch menus, bus routes, snow day notices, and links to other useful information? Would you distribute a brochure that looked like your web site?

As you know, the buck stops at your office. "The principal is ultimately responsible for everything on the school's web site," says Rence Lafond-Cantilli, who oversees Fairfax County, Virginia's 234 school web sites. Fairfax County's aim is to have a "curator" in every school who does the web work. "It's a school-by-school decision here," she says.

"A good web site can be created alone, but a great one usually cannot," says Robin McClure, communications officer for the Birdville Independent School District in Texas. The best-case scenario is to have a technical specialist in each building. Not surprisingly, many principals have delegated web site responsibility to a teacher, or let a classroom or a gung-ho parent take on the job. Most principals don't have time to review the site regularly. That's a mistake. Keep an eye on your site and memorize the address, too.

"I know that principals understand the PR and communication value of the web, but most of us don't have time to be in charge," said Pennsylvania principal Fred Brown. "The web is wonderful, but it has given us a whole new set of problems. I know that prospective parents check out web sites, but I'd really rather have them visit my school in person."

PR consultant Elliot Levine, who works on web sites for Lawrence (NY) Public Schools, recommends that web site development be a collaborative process among principals, staff, district staff, etc. "No one can build a web site alone. It changes by the minute, and the possibilities are too vast for one person," he says.

What About Security?

While researching this column, I surfed through a number of school web sites. Many were created by students; many had messages from various grade levels and photos of staff; some were very professionally designed, useful sites with messages from the principal and pop-up surveys for quick responses. Others had low-quality graphics and intrusive backgrounds; many had more than a photo of the school and a few demographics. Too many sites had kids' names, photos, and email addresses.

"Security *is* an issue," says Levine when asked about names and faces on the web. His system prints first names only and uses a standard release before any photos of students are used. Staff names and photos are handled with the same respect.

"Be careful, too, with whom you link [connect your site]," warns Lafond-Cantilli, "and go back to check on the linking sites from time to time because they change, too."

In Killeen, Texas, Principal Steve Caruson says the state law keeps them from publishing any photos or names without parental permission. His school has a site set up by the campus technologist and he finds — as do many principals — that its information is most useful to prospective parents who want to check out the school.

While most every school has an "acceptable use agreement" that parents must sign before a child uses the Internet at school, very few schools have hard and vast web policies. Baltimore County (MD) schools recently created a detailed policy that bars student last names from sites. Photos are only allowed if there are at least four youngsters in the picture, and parents sign permission slips for all student photos to be used on a site.

Develop Your Own Policy ─────────────────────────────

One Wisconsin school board has a carefully considered web policy, developed in 1996. "We were worried about publishing student works, copyright problems, and, or course, safety. So we set some parameters," says Marne Boylen, coordinator of instructional technology for Janesville (WI) Public Schools.

"When our first home page came from a teacher who used the University of Wisconsin logo upside down, we knew we had a problem," she says. Now every new site is reviewed by a committee of three, which includes the school PR person. Boylen advises caution in allowing links with alumni home pages, having people sign in and include remarks at the site's guest book, and permitting less experienced teachers to control a site's content and decide what is acceptable web fare. And of course, schools should be sure to keep parents fully informed of everything that involves their child's presence on the web.

It's a good idea for your school or district to follow Janesville's lead and develop some web guidelines.

Here's the gist of their policy:

❖ A task force forms — including students, teachers, parents, library media specialists, administrators, and so on — to create a web site.

❖ Prior to release, the task force demonstrates the site to a district review committee.

❖ Each building writes its own procedures for site monitoring, making changes to the site, and approving those changes.

❖ Copyright and privacy issues, including photos of students, student and staff directory information, and alumni addresses — receive strict attention.

❖ Only the sites that are created under this system are official representatives of the district.

"Don't be afraid of mistakes," says Elliot Levine. "We're all students in this, and there really are no rules. Sooner or later we're going to make it work for kids."

Play it safe now — it's time to start writing a few rules, especially regarding safety issues. That's good policy and good PR.

Video Programming and Cable TV

Today's audiences have grown up with television so it's only natural for you to consider using some video techniques in your communication program. Some school districts have agreements with their local cable carrier to produce and broadcast shows about their schools. Others often work with the cable companies in covering special events, such as athletic contests, graduation speeches, assemblies, and debate competitions. (For more information, see *Getting Started with Cable in the Classroom* in the resource section of this guide.)

Once again, the key is to check with your audiences to see just what they would watch on a cable station, and then work with your team to produce tapes that can work with your local station.

Seek to provide those tapes to parent groups, counselors, and real estate agents, and other interested parties. Some schools even allow them to be "rented" free of charge from the local library and video rental outlet.

It's a great way to capture extra mileage from the same production effort. Always look for ways of stretching your video production dollar.

Some additional uses of video include:

❖ Many schools now use videotapes to help parents, students, and substitute teachers become better acquainted with their new schools. Many make the tape "required viewing" before a student can officially register at the school.

❖ Some schools tape their reading instruction program to demonstrate that it uses phonics and blends in whole language. It demonstrates why both types of instruction are clearly important.

❖ To boost volunteer efforts, some schools use videos to demonstrate the varied assignments that volunteers perform in their schools. It helps to break down the stereotypical approach to volunteers and can be used in visits to corporate leaders in your attendance area to show how their employees may be able to help your school.

One final note of caution on video production is that today's audiences expect top-quality work or they'll quickly hit the remote to jump to the next station or eject your videotape. So if you want to enter this arena and deliver results, make sure you do it well.

Broadcast Fax Capabilities

Some principals use a broadcast fax system to keep the leadership of their parent groups informed or to set up a key communicators system with parents who have access to a fax machine.

This is another technique that needs to be researched to see if parents can receive faxes in their homes or at their place of work outside the home.

Email Explosion

Use of email is growing by leaps and bounds. Many parents now communicate with teachers, principals, superintendents, and board members by email.

How do busy teachers and principals effectively use email?

In focus groups around the country with parents of elementary school and middle school students, NSPRA has found email to be the up-and-coming communication device that many parents prefer. Many parents can access it from both home and work and feel that they are "connected" to their child's teachers and principal.

They appreciate the feeling of instant access and the "bureaucracy-busting" tool that email can become. One major caution is that in some socio-economic areas, many parents may not have access to email. Your research on your community should tell you whether email has a possibility of reaching a majority of your parents and other community leaders.

Planning Questions Before Implementing Email or Voice-mail Systems

Before you begin initiating an email system or a voice-mail system to bolster your community engagement program, answer the following questions to help set practical guidelines:

❖ Does staff have access to the email/voice-mail system in a comfortable setting?

❖ Can staff access the school's email/voice-mail system from home?

❖ What is the acceptable response time concerning email/voice-mail to staff?

   All email letters should normally be answered in ___ days.

   All voicemail should normally be answered in ____ days.

❖ What can be done to a parent, student, or other person who abuses the email or voice-mail system? Examples of abuse include leaving numerous messages every day, demanding instant responses, challenging the grading of papers, or using abusive language.

❖ What action will you take if some staff members do not use or abide by the email/voice-mail guidelines that you establish for your school?

❖ Does the principal need to see or have on file all email communications from the school to parents? If yes, how does that task get completed?

❖ How secure is the email/voice-mail system?

❖ When will guidelines be available for staff and parents?

❖ When will you train staff and parents about email/voicemail rules?

❖ When do you plan to do evaluate the use of email/voice-mail and possibly adjust your guidelines on its usage?

Low Power Radio

Some principals have begun a low-wattage radio station in their schools. These are the same types of systems you can tune into when you approach major metropolitan airports for parking information.

The costs may vary, but principals inform us that the cost may fall into the $1,500 to $2,000 range.

Here's how Ken Krumwided, an elementary principal in Iowa, describes his "station:"

We have the first low-wattage radio station in the country to be broadcast from an elementary school. Run by students for students, this station has a signal radius of about two miles.

Three times a day during school hours, we can tune in to continuous messages or classical music. Current features include:

- ❖ school, community, and national news;
- ❖ weather;
- ❖ the daily Pledge of Allegiance;
- ❖ sports;
- ❖ story reading and poetry;
- ❖ the lunch menu;
- ❖ a citizenship program;
- ❖ messages from the principal;
- ❖ advertisements; and
- ❖ a weekly parent program.

This idea came after a brainstorming session with our business partners who subsequently underwrote the project. The students, with help from families and school faculty and staff, sell advertisements to pay back the business partners.

Students are effectively marketing our school with the new radio station. We are all kept well-informed about campus and community activities. Job skills are taught to 5th-grade students who are trained by another local radio station. The children interview for and hold positions as general, sales, and office managers, as well as program directors.

With the help of adults in the school community, they are using and improving basic academic skills of reading, writing, speaking, and math in the ownership and operation of our successful station.

The Key to Effectively Selecting Technology

In every community engagement effort, you need to keep your target audience in mind. New technology gives you many tools to use, but you will need to select only those that will work best for your audiences.

Don't get trapped into going with something new and glamorous until you know it will work for the majority of your parents and community leaders. Keep your technology efforts as friendly, clear, and timely as you can you can make them. By doing so, your parents and other leaders will certainly enjoy their convenience and efficiency — two attributes you need to build support for your school.

Keep your technology efforts friendly, clear, and timely.

6 Communication in a Diverse World

Diversity is a growing force

Diversity is a growing force in our country and many principals have successfully engaged their multi-cultural communities by making the time to learn how to effectively reach their audiences. It is not uncommon for some principals to have more than 10 different languages spoken in their schools and some school districts must now reach students who speak more than 50 different languages.

This is one area that the busy principal has to be committed to make a difference. The challenge is to find others who can assist in helping all students be comfortable and productive in your school.

Here's how to begin reaching parents and others in a diverse community:

❖ **Seek insight from the central office and current staff**

Before embarking too far down the road, check with your central office to see how other schools may be handling translation services for non-English speaking students. Some school districts have placed translators on retainer and yours may be one of them.

Check how other schools handle translation services.

Also seek insight from your current staff — teachers, counselors, secretaries, and food service and maintenance personnel — for any contacts that they may have in helping you learn more about communicating and engaging your diverse populations.

❖ **Seek assistance from community centers and religious groups**

Key advisors to your effort will be the leaders in the community centers and religious groups in the locations housing your students. First, go to them and seek their assistance in finding ways to better reach students and parents from their area.

Ask for translation assistance in written materials, as well as translation assistance or insight for school meetings, such as Back-to-School nights, parent conferences, etc.

Also ask for insight on cultural differences that may have an impact on attendance at school, requesting extra help, etc.

Learn about any special cultural celebrations that may become a discussion item in classes in your school. Also seek permission to have meetings in their facilities for parents who may not feel comfortable coming to your school.

Community Centers or Religious Group Resources in Your Attendance Area

Language: _____

Contact: _____

Organization: _____

Address: _____

_____

_____

Phone: (_____) _____-_____

Fax: (_____) _____-_____

Email: _____

Notes: _____

_____

_____

_____

Repeat this information for each resource in your attendance area.

❖ **Establish a Liaison for Each Population**

Once you have completed the first two steps, ask for assistance in establishing a parent or community liaison for each major group.

Eventually, publicize the names of the liaisons and the fact that the principal will meet monthly with the liaison. You may choose to include the liaison in your executive committee of your parent group or school site council.

❖ **Conduct Focus Groups and Report the Results to Your Staff**

Working with the liaisons, conduct focus group in each of your communities to seek answers to the following questions:

— What is the best way for you to receive information about your child at Premiere Elementary School?

— What is the best way for you to communicate with your child's teacher? How about communicating with the principal?

— How do you find information about Premiere Elementary School?

— Have you ever attended a Back-to-School night? How about a parent conference? What can be done so you can attend? What can be done to make them more valuable for you? If free bus transportation were provided, would you attend?

— What do you like best about Premiere Elementary School? What do you feel needs to be improved?

— What cultural celebrations or practices do you wish the school to know about?

— If your child is having a problem with homework, what do you now do? What else do you think you can do? What do you think the school should do?

— If you have a question about what your child is learning, what do you do now?

— Do you have access to Internet communication? (Seek awareness about Internet communication.)

— If the school could offer a "parenting center" where you could come in and learn more about helping your child learn, would you participate? Why or why not? What if the parenting center were located in your community?

— If the school could provide a video about ways to help you help your child learn more, would you be able to play it at home? If not, would you be willing to come to the community center or church to view it? Why or why not?

It is important to share the results of these focus groups with your staff and then develop a fact sheet to help build better understanding of the diversity of your students and to make their home/school communication more effective.

One example that you may want to discuss is that many Filipino kids tend to be quiet and demure. When teachers know that, they won't automatically assume that the child is slow. A second example is that in other cultures, as a form of respect, children are taught not to look directly at you in the eye. To force them to do otherwise may cause them stress and make them less productive in your classrooms.

❖ Seek Additional Funding or Grants for Diversity Programs

Community parenting centers, paid parent liaison in schools, translation services, special training for staff and parents, and special ethnic recognition celebrations are all budget items that are not always met out of a school district's regular operating budget. Work with your central office representatives and the community centers to develop joint proposals that will fund some of these programs for your students.

❖ Attempt to Build Diversity in Your Staff

Students and parents will feel more comfortable if the ethic diversity of your staff begins to reflect your student population. It may take some time to make that happen, but ask your central office recruiters to assist you in this mission.

❖ **"This Document Is Important. Please Have It Translated!"**

If you can't have all your regular communication items translated, consider having brightly colored stickers printed in the languages you need that say, "This document is important. Please have it translated."

At least it will alert parents that important information will be missed if they do not have the information translated.

❖ **Home Visits**

Another tactic to get know one another better and build a solid home and school relationship is to visit with parents and children in their homes. Principal Lillian Brinkley in Virginia reports that she and her staff spend a great deal of time on the road for both routine visits and to talk to parents whose children are not progressing as they should. She advocates some firm rules for home visits.

"When we walk into somebody's house, we are in their kingdom. We show respect. We don't go as a person from the school, but as a friend and neighbor. We always compliment them about something in the house or the aroma of dinner on the stove," she said. And then she begins talking about their son or daughter.

❖ **Additional Considerations for Engaging and Communicating with Diverse Audiences:**

— **Welcome Centers:** Every new student must meet with a school or school district welcome center where language proficiency is assessed, the student and parents learn about life in their new school, and they also learn about additional community and school resources to help them become productive in their school.

— **Visibility at Community Events:** A principal and other staff members' attendance at ethnic and community celebrations goes a long way in demonstrating that you and your staff care about your community.

— **Welcome Posters in Many Languages**: Just translating the welcome message on your school entrance ways and classroom doors also communicates that you cared enough to make all students feel welcome. A small gesture, but a big emotional payoff.

— **Voice-Mail Translations:** Make sure that your voice-mail message is translated into the major languages in your school. At the beginning of the message, make it clear that the information will be presented in multiple languages so your caller stays on the line.

— **Specialty Media Outlets:** When you are announcing honor rolls and other reasons to celebrate, make sure you have the ethic media outlets on your media list. One of the best ways to find these outlets is to ask focus group participants what newspapers they read, what radio stations they listen to, and what television stations they watch.

 Communicating with Parents When You Don't Speak Their Language

Non-Spanish-speaking Principals Are Finding Ways to Meet the Challenge of Non-English-speaking Parents

Parent involvement is a critical element if schools are to provide a quality education for their students. As demographics change, educators are being increasingly confronted with the challenge of creating partnerships with parents who do not speak English or who have limited proficiency. According to the 1990 Census, Hispanics are the largest and fastest growing of the many and diverse ethnic and language groups in American schools.

Linguistic pluralism is fast becoming a fact of professional life for large numbers of principals. Those who do not speak Spanish must meet the challenge by developing new communication strategies to foster positive relationships between Spanish-speaking parents and their schools.

Here are some recommendations to consider:

❖ Be sure that someone on your staff is fluent in both written and oral Spanish and is available whenever an accurate translation is needed. If no staff member is qualified, request assistance from the central office. It is critical to have a professional adult do the interpreting; children should not be used, especially when confidential information is involved.

❖ Be sure that essential written materials are printed correctly in both English and Spanish. These materials include registration documents, newsletters, school announcements, and report cards. You may wish to call on parents who can read and write in Spanish to review and edit documents translated from English. They need not be fluent in English to do this.

❖ Invest in translation devices, especially for large group presentations, such as parent-teacher nights. Chapter 1 advisory meetings, and school-sponsored parent development conferences or seminars. Such devices permit parents to listen through headsets to a translator speaking in Spanish through a one-way transmitter. In communities where the dominant language is Spanish, it may be more practical to conduct meetings in Spanish while the headsets provide translation to English. In either case, be sure that you have an interpreter capable of translating simultaneously from one language to the other.

❖ Learn the language. Learn conversational Spanish as quickly as possible. Speaking the language of your school community is a great asset and reduces your dependency on others for effective communication. Some districts provide language lessons for school personnel, but even if yours doesn't, as a principal you must set an example for the rest of your staff. You might want to make bilingual fluency of all faculty and staff one of your schools' goals.

❖ Remember that the purpose of a parent conference is to communicate. Do everything possible to assist that process. Often, principals will turn a conference over to an interpreter because they feel they are not able to communicate with non-English-speaking parents. However, it is critical that the principal remain present in such situations. The unspoken message to the parents is "I care."

❖ Demonstrate interest in what parents say. Remaining attentive, despite linguistic differences, is critical. If a conference is held to make an important educational decision about a child (for special education or bilingual programs, for example), it is preferable to conduct the conference in the language the parents understand best, with a translation to English. This helps to assure the parents that their input is important and respected.

❖ Develop parent advisory committees, including Spanish speakers, to examine ways to improve communication. The committee may want to conduct interviews or surveys to learn whether information about school activities is being received by non-English-speaking parents, or why they don't attend school functions.

The committee may also be able to recommend alternative means of communication that fit the needs of your school. For example, committee members in one school make weekly calls to other parents to relay positive messages from the principal and teachers about their children. For parents without telephones, the committee mails individualized notes. Members also volunteer to be in the school office at different times during the week to ensure that Spanish translation is available when needed.

❖ Take the initiative to resolve problems. Spanish-speaking parents may feel uncomfortable in a predominantly English-speaking environment, and they may not communicate their concerns as well as they would like. By following up on their problems, you communicate your interest and generate greater comfort levels in later meetings. Parents will often confide in a staff member they know and trust. If so, make sure that your staff understands that every parental concern is your concern, and that such information should be relayed to you immediately.

❖ Be visible in areas or activities that provide the greatest community contact. Not all Hispanic parents attend football games or board meetings. Seek opportunities to meet them outside the traditional school environments at festivals, celebrations, concerns, dances, or food drives. A principal in a border community makes it a point to do his family's grocery shopping in the vicinity of his school rather than his home, and feels that this visibility has made him more readily accepted by the community.

❖ Work with the central office and school board to promote language development programs for school personnel and parents. Many colleges and universities provide low-cost Spanish language courses, often at sites in the district, as well as summer studies in Spanish-speaking countries. On the other hand, English as a Second Language (ESL) evening programs should be available in your school building for parents and community members who want to learn English.

❖ Respect the language and culture. Do not discourage parents who are learning to speak English (and even those who are bilingual) from speaking in Spanish to their children. Some principals feel that limiting the use of Spanish or recommending an English-only policy in the home will translate into higher test scores. But studies show that such practices have not raised test scores, nor have they improved the school's academic or social ambience for parent and child. A more effective approach is to encourage and honor the language and culture of the home, while providing the best possible ESL programs.

It is essential for educators to diversify their modes of communication, become more attuned to the cultural realities of the changing school community, and develop programs and policies that enhance communication between the school and the community. The success of non-Spanish-speaking principals will depend on how well they learn to communicate with non-English-speaking parents.

Principals in the Public

Special Projects
and Opportunities

Special Projects and Opportunities

Parent-Teacher Conferences

All schools have meetings at which teachers update parents on the progress of their youngsters. These meetings are opportunities for your school to establish a reputation of caring for both the students and their parents. Review with your teachers the importance of these meetings in developing support for your school.

❖ **Timing is an important consideration.** With more and more parents working, many may have difficulty attending conferences during the school day. Some principals ask business partners to write letters to other business colleagues, stressing the value of these conferences and urging employers to give parents time off to attend these conferences without penalty.

Meeting time can also be a topic at civic club presentations and for religious leaders to communicate. If that approach does not work, consider scheduling some parent-teacher conferences in the evening.

❖ ***Impressions count.*** Make sure that teachers are aware of parents' first impressions when they enter the classroom. If the teacher is slumped in a chair behind the desk, one impression will be delivered. If the teacher greets parents warmly at the classroom door with a smile and handshake, another impression is communicated.

❖ ***Give parents what they want.*** Teachers should:

— focus on information that is important to parents,

— stay away from educational jargon,

— have plenty of examples of students' work,

— leave ample time for parent questions,

— urge that parents ask questions, and

— commend the parents for working with students.

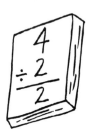

It's helpful for teachers to suggest how parents can support what's going on in the classroom. Parent-teacher conferences are a great time to distribute tips on how parents can help their children. If important dates are scheduled, such as due dates for projects, testing times, or major field trips, teachers should remind parents of them.

If a student seems to be struggling, the teacher should suggest specific activities that the student, parents, and teacher could do to improve the situation. Parents can certainly share this responsibility, and teachers should point out the value of the parent-teacher partnership.

➤ Idea for Action

If teachers are serious about being positive communicators for the school, they should identify two or three parents and phone them a few days after the conference to ask what they liked and what they didn't like. This practice is especially important for young teachers, but it always helps to see how our communications are received. Teachers don't need to share this

evaluation with you; they only need to use it to identify ways to make their conferences stronger.

➤ **Idea for Action**

Many new teachers say that they were never taught how to conduct a parent-teacher conference. Consider having veteran teachers role-play a good parent-teacher conference for rookie teachers. They can also role-play *Some of My Most Embarrassing Moments in Conferences* or talk about the typical questions parents ask.

❖ ***Help teachers gain confidence for parent conferences.*** Parents and teachers have common goals. Both:

— want children to succeed,

— want children to progress at the rate best for them,

— want children to feel that the standards at home and at school complement each other,

— believe that learning takes place at school and at home, and

— believe that the school curriculum is the beginning that leads to much more that is worthwhile for children to learn.

❖ ***Help teachers develop conference skills.***

— Prepare carefully and ensure privacy.

— Provide an informal setting and establish rapport.

— Set a time limit.

— Begin on a positive note.

— Encourage the parents to talk and listen attentively.

— Develop an attitude of mutual cooperation.

— Delay making numerous definite suggestions yourself.

— Encourage suggestions from the parents.

— Use parents' practical suggestions as a springboard for action.

— Summarize the points covered and make plans together for future progress.

— End on a note of continuing cooperation.

— Make notes after parents leave.

— Be informed about school purposes, methods, and achievements.

❖ *What parents want to know:*

— Is my child doing as well as he or she should be? Is he or she working to his ability?

— What group is my child in and why? (Explain ability grouping.)

— What kind of books are you using? (Show some and explain why.)

— May I see some of the work? (Show some, preferably from a file which will show progress and changes.)

— Does he or she get along well with others? (If not, tell in what ways. Don't use a flat *No*. Try to describe some ways in which the student works well with others.)

— Have you noticed any special interests, aptitudes, or abilities in my child? (Approach this question cautiously, but be honest. Cite any special interests you've noticed. It may help the parent to work better with the child at home.)

— Does the child obey? Does the child respect others?

— Have you noticed any signs of initiative, originality, or responsibility in the classroom? (Try to name some.)

— How is the child getting along in individual subjects?

— How can I help at home?

— What is my child's IQ? (Explain in terms of average, above average. Be sure that you know your school district's policy on releasing information about IQ scores.)

— Does my child get to class on time? Does my child eat lunch?

— Is it all right to call you at home?

Don't be shocked if a seemingly routine question pops up, like:

— What time does school start?
— Are behavior traits filed with the cumulative record?
— What is an IQ?

And make sure that, if a teacher doesn't know the answer to a question, he or she admits it and promises to find and call with the answer.

❖ **What teachers can hope to learn:**

— What is the child's reaction to school? Is there something the child especially likes or dislikes? Does the child feel able to do the work?

— How is the child's health? What recent illness, disability, or accident has he had? Are there any problems with sleep, bad dreams, awakening early?

— How is the child's emotional adjustment? Are there any things that are troubling? Under what conditions does the child seem worried or fearful? Does the child's self-confidence need bolstering? How does the child react to not getting what he wants?

— How does the child spend time out of school?

— What hobbies, special interests, and abilities have been shown at home?

— What is the child's response to rules and regulations in the home?

— What discipline works best with the child at home?

— Does the child have any at home responsibilities?

— Does the child have a suitable place to read or work?

❖ *Avoid using negative expressions.*

Avoid negative expressions.

Instead of this...	Try this...
lazy	can do more when he tries
troublemaker	disturbs class
uncooperative	should learn to work with others
stupid	can do better work with help
never does the right thing	can learn to do the right thing
impertinent	is discourteous
stubborn	insists on having his own way
sloppy	could do neater work
liar	doesn't always tell the truth
mean	has difficulty getting along with others
failed	failed to meet the requirements
poor grade of work	is working below his standard
rude	is inconsiderate of others
show-off	tries to get attention

❖   **Prepare, then relax.** You'll want to have plenty of information on hand about each pupil in your class. Get together the cumulative record folders, recent tests, health records, and all other available data for pre-conference review.

You should know each child's ability in terms of average, superior, and so on (parents often have trouble interpreting IQ's accurately). Be ready to tell the parent if the child is working up to grade level and where he or she is weak or strong.

— Prepare a folder of each student's work to give to the parents. Include samples of work done in every subject from the beginning of the semester until conference time.

On the outside of the folder, write a brief comment about the child's progress. These folders will help you cover the fundamentals and, if you don't have time to cover everything during the conference, the parent can read the material at home. And if both parents don't come to the conference, the folder will help one parent fill the other in on the details.

— Make a check sheet of the various skills and attitudes that you want to discuss during the conference. The list will keep the conference moving and help you remember all the important points you want to cover.

— Consider making a tape recording of each pupil's work during a reading lesson. You can open the conference by asking the parents whether they would like to hear the child read. They will, of course! The tape is an icebreaker that gets the conference off to a good start.

— Plan your schedule so that you'll have a 5-10 minute breather after each conference to jot down notes and assemble materials for the next set of parents. This will save both you and the parents from feeling that you're caught in a perpetual motion assembly line.

End on an optimistic note.

— The conference which you began with
  encouraging news should end on a note of optimism. For example, say, "I'm so
  glad, Mrs. Taylor, that you suggested helping Karen make the sounds book for use
  at home. I'm sure it will help her with her reading."

— Summarize major areas discussed.

— Agree on action needed.

— Clarify the next steps.

— Extend an invitation to visit school any time.

— See the parents to the door — allow yourself a 10-minute
  interlude, if possible — and welcome the next ones in with
  a smile, even if the last conference was a problem.

Organization is the key to a successful parent conference

Subject areas and topics: Write down the topics you intend to cover.

Major objectives: What do you hope to accomplish? What do you need to communicate? What do you want to communicate?

Conference plan: What steps can you follow during the conference to ensure that you meet your major objectives? What questions will you ask? What points will you make? What suggestions will you offer? Will you allow time for parents to ask questions and make comments?

Materials: What materials should be shared with parents? Are they organized to complement your conference plan?

Action plan: How can you wind up the conference with a plan for action? Will you recommend any specific steps? Do you have suggestions on ways parents can work with you?

Review: Summarize what has been said during the conference. (Tell parents what you've already told them.) End with a friendly thanks to the parents. Tell them it's nice to work with parents who are interested in their child's education.

Evaluation: After the conference, ask yourself these questions:

— Was I prepared? Did I use time well?

— Did I have an informal setting and ensure privacy?

— Did I begin on a positive note? Did I encourage parents to talk and offer suggestions?

— Did I listen attentively? Did I plan with the parents?

— Did I learn anything new to help me teach the child?

— If I had the chance, what would I do differently?

Help Parents Prepare for Their Teacher Conferences

Parents should also have a plan to get the most from their conference. How about providing them with this checklist?

❖ **Tips for Parents**

Before the conference

✔ Have I decided on specific questions to ask the teacher? For example, is our child doing as well as expected in reading? Why are certain procedures followed in the classroom? What are the policies regarding homework?

✔ Am I prepared to answer questions that might be asked by the teacher about my child's hobbies and interests? Special health problems? Provisions for study at home?

✔ Have I expressed interest in the conference with my child? Have I noted an especially good experience or problem area my child has had in school to relate to the teacher? Have I asked my child if he or she has questions or complaints?

After the conference

❖ Note the important points of the conference.

❖ Share the results of the conference with your child.

❖ Together design a definite action plan that will promote improved academic growth for your child.

❖ Feel free to arrange additional conferences.

A Special Invitation for the Parent Conference

A letter from the teacher sets the tone for the conference. Consider a letter like this one:

Dear Parent:

You and I are going to talk about someone very special next week -- of course, it is your child. When we meet at parent-teacher conferences, I'll talk about:

❖ How your child is doing,

❖ What we've done and what we plan to do in our class.

❖ How you and I can work together as partners to provide the best possible education for your child.

You probably have some things you'd like to talk about, too — like homework, how you can help at home, and perhaps, school policies. It helps if you write down the things you want to discuss before you come to the conference. That's why I've left some space below. Write down questions and comments you have. Then bring this note with you to our meeting.

Questions you have about your child:

_____

_____

Our action plan-- After our conference, there may be some things we can do to better serve your child. We'll write those below during our meeting.

_____

_____

Thanks for helping me with your child.

Your Child's Teacher

Finding Out If Your Conference Was a Success

A parent survey can help you and your teachers determine if conferences were meaningful. You may want to ask questions like these to help you and your staff plan for the next round of conferences.

1. All things considered, how would you rate your parent-teacher conference?
   - ❑ Excellent
   - ❑ Good
   - ❑ Average
   - ❑ Poor

2. What part of the conference was most helpful to you?

3. How could we have improved the conference?

4. What kinds of information about our school would you like to see in our newsletter?

5. Are there any general comments you'd like to make about our schools?

6. Did the conference help you better understand your child's progress?
   - ❑ Yes
   - ❑ No   Please explain _____
     _____

   Do you feel you had an adequate opportunity to contribute to the school's understanding of your child?
   - ❑ Yes
   - ❑ No   Please explain _____
     _____

7. What grade is your child (or children) in?
   - ❑ Kindergarten, first, second
   - ❑ Third, fourth
   - ❑ Fifth, sixth

The Question

A tremendous amount of information is communicated to parents when **The Question** is asked. Especially at the elementary level, parents will ask their youngsters almost every night,

What did you do at school today?

We sometimes joke about the response to that question, but it's a legitimate aspect of your school's public relations program and a very credible piece of communication. You can help create more positive answers to that question in two ways:

❖ *Get parents to ask the right question.* To encourage a meaningful answer, parents might ask, *"What was the most exciting thing you learned at school today?"* or *"Tell me one new thing you learned today."* If parents really want to learn what occurred, they shouldn't simply ask a single question and let it go at that. They should ask follow-up questions, focusing on subjects or on different times of the school day. It also makes sense for parents to share an aspect of their day with their child so this session becomes a communication activity and not a grilling of the student.

❖ *Encourage teachers to prepare students for the answer to this question* that they know will come. At the end of the day, elementary teachers should summarize with students what was actually taught. In middle school, teachers should make sure students understand the objectives of the lessons so they can explain the importance of what is being learned.

➤ Ideas for Action:  One elementary school teacher has students spend the last 10 minutes of each day writing in their personal journal on the subject, "What I learned today." Students leave the school with that information fresh in their minds, with the hope that they remember it when their parents ask **The Question**. This can be a language arts assignment if the teacher wants to collect the journals and read them, or it can remain between each student and her or his journal.

"This Week's News"

Date: __Sept. 7__

Dear __Mom and Dad__

In math we are studying

addition and 2 place addition. We took an addition pre-test today.

Here is an example of the kind of problems we worked on this week:

$$25 \quad 49 \quad 15$$
$$+32 \quad -26 \quad +76$$

In reading
I read to my teacher and worked on base words

In social studies we are learning about
maps and globes

In health we are learning
what happens when you smoke

Some interesting things I've done this week are:
following written directions and writing animal stories

Love from

Tom

Tips for Back-to-School Night

Let's start with a show of hands...

How many of you attended the recent Back-to-School Night at your elementary or middle school?

How many returned home that evening feeling great about a majority of the teachers and the school? How many of you thought, *Geez, this could be so much better, if only they would...*

How do we get better at Back-to-School nights? Some of the following tips may help. They are based on years of attending these functions as a parent, mixed with some common sense communication advice based on a career in professional communication.

❖ ***Give an Enthusiastic Welcome.*** Principals need to be enthusiastic in their welcome so that infectious enthusiasm sets the tone for the evening. In addition to welcoming parents and others, thank them for choosing your school. Today's parents have more options than ever, and an acknowledgment that you are pleased to have their children and that you will do all you can to make it a great year for them will start the year off on a good note — a major objective for the evening.

❖ ***Give 'Em Something to Brag About.*** Just about every parent would love to have some great facts to gloat about when talking about their kids' schools and especially when they are chatting with parents who are sending their kids to Stellar Prep. Academic achievements, depth and range of classes offered, credentials and accolades of staff, and success stories of past students all fit into this important category. Remember, if you don't give them this information, who else will?

❖ ***Train Teachers.*** Most staff members have never been coached on parent-friendly procedures for Back-to-School nights, and some say that their fear of

facing a classroom of parents ranks up there with a scheduled root canal procedure. In your training, consider the following:

— **Greet Parents Right Outside Your Door.** Make eye contact, shake their hands, welcome and thank them for coming. Make it a "quickie" so parents can get to their seats. Over the years, some teachers had sign-up sheets outside the door, lines formed, and some parents missed half of the teacher's presentation. Not a great way to build confidence in your classroom management abilities.

— **Plan, Time, and Practice Your Presentation** — Twelve minutes is twelve minutes. If you have 12 minutes, plan for it. More often than not, the bell rings, teachers say, "I can't believe that's all the time I had," and then add, "if you have any questions, contact me," and never tell parents how.

Practice your 12-minute presentation. To blurt out, "I can't believe…" makes parents question your ability to plan regular lessons and your overall time management skills. *(The worst example of this is when poor management is still happening by the 5th period class that same evening.)*

With pertinent information on a hand-out, your 12 minutes can be easily spent talking about how glad you are to teach their children and the major items you will cover this year. Most parents do not want to hear about the state or district standards; they just want to know what you will be teaching their kids this year, and you want to leave them with the impression that their kids are in great hands for English, math, science, etc.

— **Enthusiasm for Students and Subjects Is a Must — Scratch the Ferris Bueller Teacher Monotone.** Always remember that just about every parent went to school; they sit in front of you with their image of a great teacher. And most likely, their "great teacher profile" was one painted with a caring attitude for students, their love of their subject, and their ability to make the subject connect with their students.

And remember that enthusiasm can go a long way in making a great first impression on Back-to-School nights. Don't let parents return home agreeing with their son that you are the second-coming of Ferris Bueller's teacher. You need to be yourself, but turn up the "enthusiasm volume" a notch or two during Back-to-School night.

— ***Make Sure You Give Them a Hand-out.*** During my years in business communication, a hand-out or "leave-behind" was mandated because it reinforces the message of the presentation. If customers missed something during the presentation, they could refer to the leave-behind and even contact you for follow-up or, hopefully, further business.

Every teacher needs to distribute a hand-out that covers:

— the presentation,
— topics to be taught,
— special projects,
— deadlines,
— amount and philosophy of homework,
— class expectations, and
— grading.

You also need to list communication contact numbers and your preferred times and method of communication. List your e-mail address, voice-mail number, and other methods of contacting you.

Make sure parents know you are willing to give "extra-help" sessions to students and, again, communicate the best ways for students to ask for that help. Demonstrate your commitment to helping your students learn and make sure that you communicate that you expect the same commitment from your students and the "home."

— ***Killer Phrases to Avoid and Why.*** Here's a listing of phrases to avoid… the rationale, from a parent's perspective, seems self-evident:

"I'm sorry; I don't have enough handouts." (Once again, a sign of botched planning.)

"Your kids are great, many of them know more about _____ than I do." (Fill in the blank with technology, or worse, the teacher's subject matter, and some parents will begin questioning why you are their child's teacher.)

"See me after this session for more information," (But that means I'll miss the next teacher's session or be late for it and your next "12-minute" period will begin late.)

"I don't know what we will be teaching next week." (The truth does hurt.)

"I'm not sure what all these standardized tests are really for… and our principal doesn't either." (Don't talk about things you don't know and, if questioned, give parents insight on where to get further help.)

"I was given this class to teach because they couldn't find anyone else to teach it." (Not a confidence booster for most parents.)

Remember that Back-to-School night is one of the key impression/reputation-building moments each school has. You can make it into a reputation builder or breaker — the choice is yours.

Rich Bagin, APR
Executive Director
NSPRA

From the October 1999 issue of *NSPRA Network*

Surviving Back-to-School Night

I am a veteran of 39 Back-to-School Nights (BTSN), 17 as a parent, 16 as a teacher, and 6 as an administrator. While I have approached them with varied expectations, I've found that they all have one thing in common — the potential to make or break the parent-teacher relationship. Parents' first impressions often affect a teacher's credibility. We've all heard horror stories of poor presentations by competent teachers who pay the price for parents' negative perceptions for the rest of the year — or for their careers. Yet, preparation for this all-important night is often reduced to a memo reminding staff about what time they should report!

The purpose of the teacher's BTSN presentation is to explain the objectives of instruction; outline the curriculum; set expectations; explain grading, attendance and homework policies; and answer questions — all within 10 minutes. Obviously, teachers must reduce their presentations to essential information that parents need to know.

Selling Yourself

Good presentations involve good salesmanship. But selling your teaching expertise, your instructional program, and your enthusiasm for your school and your students in the brief time available takes considerable preparation — and some common sense. For example, when a parent walks into a child's classroom and has to take a chair off a table to sit down, the message is that this classroom is not a welcoming environment. It is a message that the parents may pass on to their children.

Parents love to see examples of their children's work displayed on Back-to-School Night, and they especially appreciate it when teachers show that they know their child. I remember how my son's middle school art teacher placed student work on tables and, as parents entered the room, she encouraged them to find their children's pictures. If a parent couldn't find the picture, the teacher immediately identified it. Her familiarity with each student's work send parents a powerful message that she knew and cared about their children.

An important lesson for teachers on Back-to-School Night is to sell what they are doing and not apologize for what they are *not* doing. One of my children had a wonderful teacher of World Studies. But on Back-to-School Night, he began his presentation with an apology.

Because he didn't have the time to send home weekly computerized reports as in years past, the reports would be sent only every other week. The parents were clearly disappointed. But if he had simply told the parents they could expect a comprehensive, individualized grade report every two weeks, the response would have been overwhelmingly positive.

A common mistake teachers make in BTSN presentations is to wave a textbook in the air, identifying it as the one students will be using in class. This tells parents nothing but the color of the cover. But taking time to explain the textbook's contents, organization, and merits gives parents important information. Some teachers even point out how parents can use review questions at the end of chapters to quiz their children before tests.

Preparing for the Worst

Parents come to Back-to-School Night for a variety of reasons. Some are just curious to put a face with a name. Others want to please their children by getting involved with school. Most are genuinely interested in meeting teachers and hearing about their curriculums and expectations. But a few come with negative agendas, and occasionally a parent may verbally assault a teacher. Teachers can avoid confrontational situations by maintaining their composure and inviting these parents to discuss their specific concerns at private meetings.

Principals are responsible for ensuring that teachers are properly prepared for Back-to-School Night, and a staff meeting for this purpose can be informative and even enjoyable. A few years ago, concerned about negative statements made by some staff members during the previous year's BTSN, we came up with an ingenious way to demonstrate what teachers should *not* do at BTSN.

We recruited the drama teacher to prepare a script and he enlisted staff members to play the roles of teacher and parents. When the teachers arrived for the staff meeting, they were greeted by the role-playing teacher as though they were parents entering his classroom on Back-to-School Night. A banner across the blackboard gave his name and the misspelled title of his course. He then proceeded to make every possible mistake, including comments like: "Welcome to my worst class," and "You must be Joey's father — he's as fat as you are."

The planted "parents" asked questions, each of which received an inappropriate response. While everyone laughed through the "presentation," they got the point we were trying to make. As a result, we had out most positive BTSN ever.

Another tactic we have used to prepare teachers for Back-to-School Night is to list presentation dos and don'ts. Here are some examples:

Do

❖ Introduce yourself.
❖ Ask parents to identify themselves.
❖ Be positive and confident.
❖ Display student work.
❖ Discuss homework and grading.
❖ Discuss instructional and grouping practices.
❖ Tell parents to call if they have any concerns.

Don't

❖ Tell parents you are looking forward to retirement.
❖ Ask parents if this child is as dumb as their last one.
❖ Hold up the textbook without any explanation.
❖ Say that you like to keep kids guessing about their grades.
❖ Say that this is the worst or largest class you've ever had.
❖ Say that you have a hard time keeping kids' names straight.
❖ Bad mouth the administration.

Being prepared, confident, and armed with a smile is the best way to approach Back-to-School Night, which should be regarded as an ideal opportunity to showcase the school as well as the teachers' energy, enthusiasm, knowledge, and love of children. Last year, an hour before Back-to-School Night was to begin, I had a conversation with a new teacher who had just completed his first three weeks in the classroom. When I asked if he was ready, he grinned and said, "I was born ready!" That's the kind of attitude we'd like to see in all of our teachers on every Back-to-School Night.

Carole C. Goodman
Principal
Montgomery County (Md.)

From the September 1995 issue of *Principal*

Customer-Friendly Schools: Making a Good First Impression

First Impressions Are Important — From the Outside Looking in

Imagine you are driving through a community for the first time. You notice that the public buildings are attractive and appear to be well maintained. You begin to realize that this is a community where people take pride in their municipal facilities. The library, town hall, public parks, recreational facilities all appear to be in top-notch condition. You get the feeling that people care about their community. You assume the town is well managed and a good place to live.

It is much the same with the schools. When they have the look of being cared for, it is assumed that the schools are in good hands. People assume that the inside is also cared for — and that includes the students, the files, the instructional program, the equipment, and the entire facility. If the entrance to the school is littered with trash, surrounded with graffiti, and has a general rundown appearance — people begin to wonder whether attention is given to other management details. And they wonder if their child should go to that school.

It is important to discuss this subject with the school staff and listen for agreement and concern that perhaps this subject is more important than they had realized.

Let's begin with the welcome sign. Is it friendly? Was it purchased from a school supply catalog? Was it created by a student? Sometimes the welcome sign directs visitors to report to the office. That can be done with friendly words or it can read like a stern order. "Please come to the office so we can welcome you and give you a visitor badge. That is much better that simply stating, "All visitors must report to the office."

What do we see as we look around the entrance to your school?

Do we see green shrubs and flowers? Do we see potted shrubs that are moved in and out each day? Do we see a ragged flag or a crisp new flag? Do we see old litter in the corners — or occasional new litter? (There is a big difference between old litter and new litter). Everyone

can excuse new litter that is hours old. Most of us cannot accept that we must live with litter that has been there for months or years.)

We need to be sure we have a daily clean-up scheduled and performed. At many elementary schools, the custodian begins the day by walking around the front of the school or the entire building and picking up the new litter that was dropped during the past 24 hours.

Use the following walk-through checklist to maintain a positive appearance for your building:

Walk-through Checklist for Principal and Head Custodian

Let's begin at the main entrance and walk around the area before we go into the building. Let's imagine that we are the superintendent and board president on a weekend visit to district facilities. What will we see?

❖ Any litter and trash in the entrance area?

❖ Any old weeds? Any old leaves?

❖ Have shrubs been trimmed to attractive size?

❖ Any dangerous cracks in sidewalk or steps?

❖ Graffiti on front entrance or surrounding area?

❖ Is there evidence of "old litter" around doors and corners?

❖ Are there work needs that require the help of central facilities staff?

❖ Are the entrance halls clear of cartons and unused furniture?

❖ Are the drinking fountains clean and inviting?

❖ Are all lighting fixtures working properly?

❖ Are the mop closets and equipment supply rooms tidy and clean?

❖ Is the custodians' office clean and orderly?

Once You Approach the Front Door...

Now that we have reviewed the normal upkeep and maintenance areas, it's time to play the role of the new parent coming to register in your building. What do I see as first impressions and what do those impressions tell me about your building?

The following checklist was designed to help you see your school from the eyes of the new parent and student:

Walk-Through Checklist for Principal and Faculty Representatives

❖ Is the welcome sign friendly?

❖ Student art display?

❖ Student work on display?

❖ Hallways clean?

❖ Directions to office?

❖ Cordial and professional greeting from secretary?

❖ Feeling that you are about to be "taken care of?"

❖ Secretary workplace tidy?

❖ Secretary name on display?

❖ Lack of clutter and attractive surroundings?

❖ Fresh plants or flowers?

❖ Business-like atmosphere?

❖ Visitor packet available?

❖ Floor plan for orientation to building?

❖ Pamphlet rack for parents to take publications?

❖ Place for visitors to sit while they wait for appointment?

Secretaries Are Key to a Customer-Friendly School

A friendly and happy elementary school secretary is the best public relations person any school can claim. The secretary is almost always the first person to greet a visitor or new family coming to register a child for school.

The first visit to the school often establishes the tone of the relationship between the school staff and the family. The school secretary is either an image builder or an image breaker. Principals need to make sure they have the right person for this very "public" position.

When visitors, parents, and children are greeted warmly and sincerely, the school is immediately seen as a friendly place where children will be happy. If the secretary is slow to greet visitors, abrupt, or appearing to be overworked and disorganized — the visitors will wonder if others in the school suffer under similar circumstances.

The secretarial workstation should be orderly and attractive. It should be a workplace — uncluttered and efficient. The secretary should be skilled at greeting visitors, answering the phone, and asking a child or teacher to wait a minute — all at the same time.

There are ways to do this and the elementary principal should help the school secretary to be friendly and efficient.

School Secretary Customer-Friendly Checklist

School secretaries should master a few work habits that will make the job easier. The following checklist may be helpful:

❖ Keep phone conversations short.

❖ Limit personal phone calls.

❖ Keep a personal school "Information Resource" guidebook handy, including all the forms, calendars, and procedures you need during the course of the day.

❖ Alert the principal when you notice a trend developing from a series of requests from parents and staff.

❖ Always use the hold button when juggling calls.

❖ Refer calls to others or take messages for return calls during busy times.

❖ Establish a routine for the day.

❖ Keep visiting time to a minimum.

❖ Don't volunteer to assist with projects unless time to complete them is certain.

❖ Clear the desk of unfinished work at the end of each day.

❖ Be willing to take work home when absolutely required — but never routinely.

❖ Avoid gossip and getting involved in the business of others.

❖ Look organized, even when you feel your world is coming apart.

❖ Show parents you understand their request, even though you do not have the authority to grant it.

❖ Always be polite and professional.

❖ Arrange work by seasons, weeks, and daily tasks. Make a plan and work the plan.

❖ Make sure everyone knows when you are working to meet a deadline. Everyone should understand and respect deadlines.

❖ Keep smiling and polite through it all. A smile can melt anger nearly every time.

The Welcome Packet and Welcome Center: A Powerful Customer-Friendly Tool

When you are new to a community or school, you normally want to learn as much as you can as soon as you can. Developing a welcome packet that answers most questions is a great way to greet new students and parents.

The contents of the packet can also be placed on your school's website so that you can easily refer parents to it when they have lost their original packet.

Some schools have also started welcome centers that greet parents by appointment. Normally staffed by parent volunteers, the new parents make an appointment to sit and chat with other parents who know and enjoy the school. They can run through the welcome packet and answer any questions the parents may have about their new school and community.

Welcome Packet Checklist

Use the following checklist to develop a packet for new staff, new families, and visitors to the school. Your school handbook or parent handbook will include much of this information.

Consider what publications are available from the school district for inclusion in each packet. You may want three versions — one for new staff, one for new families, and one for visitors. Remember, a generic welcome packet is better than none.

Include the following:

❖ Welcome letter from principal, parent group president, faculty representative

❖ Curriculum for each grade level

❖ Floor plan for school

❖ Plot plan for school grounds and surrounding neighborhood (streets and adjoining landmarks)

❖ Calendar for the school year

❖ School hours

❖ Parent group meetings/volunteering in school

❖ Fund-raising events

❖ Note about assistance for non-English speaking parents and students

❖ Parenting classes

❖ Report cards, state assessments, student placement

❖ Transportation schedules

❖ What to do when you have a complaint

❖ School district and school website addresses

❖ Staff list (names, titles, room numbers, office phone extensions, e-mail addresses)

❖ School district administrator list with titles, phone numbers, and e-mail addresses

❖ History of the school – date built, dates remodeled, awards, etc.

❖ Staff bios – brief, friendly, warm, human – not only college degrees

❖ Library – number of books, technology, evening hours, services

❖ Cafeteria – breakfast (costs), lunch (costs), free lunch program

❖ Homework expectations, field trips, special events

Principal for a Day

The best way to shape an individual's attitudes is through personal experience, and that is the point to a Principal for a Day program. The idea is to identify a community leader who may not understand the rigors of your job or the challenges educators face today, and invite that person to shadow you for a full day.

Schools have included business leaders, state legislators, and even newspaper reporters as a Principal for a Day. Make your selection strategic so your "guest principal" can add his or her stature, clout, credibility, or celebrity to your school.

The value of this activity was demonstrated by one business leader who spent a day in a Los Angeles elementary school and left by saying, "Gee, schools today are being asked to do everything." A newsletter article discussing the myriad tasks educators perform would not have made the impact that the personal visit did.

To initiate a Principal for a Day program,

- ❖ Identify people to approach,
- ❖ Send them a letter with the basic information, and
- ❖ Follow up with a phone call.

Encourage them to participate in the entire day. If you generally arrive at school at 6:30 A.M. and make coffee, so should the bank president as Principal for a Day.

These people may not be willing to attend your evening events, but make sure that they know about them. And Principals for Day are not allowed to attend a two-hour business lunch if you have cafeteria duty.

Some people wonder whether the Principal for a Day can be included in a discipline or other hearing with a student and parent. This can happen only if the parent agrees. But make sure that the Principal for a Day understands beforehand that situations may develop where he or she has to be excluded for legal reasons.

This concept can also work for others in the school. For instance, you might consider Student for a Day programs to alert people to the tough work that students are doing (Be

sure to schedule a day when tests are being given), or you might think about trying a Teacher for a Day program.

You may also want to attempt to receive some press coverage for the Principal of the Day activity. Inform the media about a week ahead of the day and give background on your selected candidate. Let them know that there will be "photo opportunities" so the media sees it as a possible feature story. Let them know that the "Principal for a Day" will also be happy to interview with them about what it was like to be principal in your elementary school.

If the media does not pick up on your request, make sure that someone jots down the comments by your guest principal so you can use them in your newsletters and websites.

Accountability

The accountability issue is growing stronger every year.

State assessments, report cards, and school profiles by the state, central office, major media, and consumer watchdog groups all seem to find a way to rank your school. Some parents come "armed" to meetings with the latest curriculum innovations they just received from surfing on the web. Others want to know how you are teaching reading and if you offer pre- and post- school activities. And one group of parents wants to know how much longer they will have to put up with an "obviously" weak teacher who is just coasting out to her retirement planned for two years from now.

As principal, you know what's working and what's not. You also know that testing is not the only way to evaluate how your school is doing. So it is time to become pro-active in proving that your school is continuously improving. And in those rare cases where it is not improving, it's time to communicate what you are doing about it.

The accountability issue means that you must be pro-active. Don't wait for others to tell you how bad or good your school is. (And when was the last time a group told you how good your school was — unless you won a national or state blue ribbon award? And even that process called for you to be pro-active by completing the lengthy paperwork just to be considered for the award.)

If you don't provide leadership on the accountability issue, who else will tell your story? And who knows your building better than you do?

One of the major accountability vehicles principals face today is the school profile or report card. Many are driven by state information, but it a great time to tell your side of the story to all your key audiences. Listed below is a checklist for school profiles followed by some recent information about what parents prefer when reading school profiles:

School Profile Checklist

❖ Do more than the minimum of state requirements. Just use the state guidelines as a starting point. This is one time that your parents and others will focus on your school. Take advantage of it and tell your school's story. If you must follow the state report format, bury the state report in your own school profile. Use your profile as a "wrap" for the state's profile. Make yours attractive and easy to read. Chances are good that the state report will be less readable.

❖ View the issuing of your school's profile as one of the major communication events for your year.

❖ Throughout the report, highlight key messages of what your school stands for. *Example*: Top-Flight Readers Make the Difference!

❖ Give third-party anecdotal accounts of how great your school really is. Include comments from parents, visiting dignitaries, and community leaders.

❖ Highlight awards that your school, students, and staff have received.

❖ Highlight results and anecdotes of accomplishments of students and staff. "Third grade teacher Marci Shultz has led sessions on math instruction for third grade teachers throughout the state during the past year. Marci's excellence has always been recognized by our parents and students, but it's great to see Premiere Elementary being recognized throughout the state."

❖ Give parents and others something to brag about. Most parents want to say good things about their child's school. Make sure you include two or three items in your school profile. Offer a "We're Proud of…" section.

❖ Show the range of great things your school does, as well as your test scores. Be reminded of the "softer side" of school by also listing all the wonderful art, music, and civic opportunities your kids accomplished.

❖ Use your school profile as an orientation and recruitment vehicle for your school.

❖ Break out the test score progress of students who have been with your school for 3-5 years.

❖ Highlight the academic background of your staff – colleges attended, papers written, honors, etc.

❖ Highlight accomplishments of past students.

❖ Use photos of children and academic work.

❖ Remind readers of parent and adult responsibilities to make **their** school a success.

❖ Show the enrichment opportunities at your school.

❖ Weave in the technology enhancements of the past year and what it means for your students.

❖ Add items from a brainstorming session of your staff and parent group on "What we are most proud of at our school."

Some Interesting Research on School Profiles/Report Cards

A Plus Communications based in Arlington, Virginia, has conducted some preliminary research through focus groups and other data-gathering devices to see how parents feel about the content of school report cards and school profiles. Some of the results are below.

But it would also be important to know what your parents and your community would like to see in these report cards. Conduct focus groups of your own or at least have a discussion with the executive committee of your parent group, your staff, and school site council to see what they think these reports should include.

The chart on the following page shows how parents, taxpayers, and educators rated 21 possible indicators that could be reported to hold schools accountable. They rated these indicators on a scale of 0 to 10, with 10 being most important. The indicators are arranged according to what parents say is most important (top) to least important (bottom).

Possible indicators that could be reported to hold schools accountable			
Using a scale of 1 to 10			
Category	*Parents*	*Taxpayers*	*Educators*
School safety	9.6	9.4	9.3
Teacher qualifications	9.3	9.2	8.3
Class size	8.9	7.9	8.8
Graduation rates	8.7	8.2	8.3
Dropout rates	8.3	8.1	7.4
Statewide test scores	8.2	8.0	7.1
Parental satisfaction survey data	8.1	8.0	7.0
SAT/ACT scores	8.1	7.9	6.9
Percent of students promoted to next grade	8.0	8.1	7.0
Course offerings	7.8	7.9	7.3
Attendance rates	7.8	8.0	7.6
Per-pupil spending	7.6	7.6	8.0
Student satisfaction survey data	6.5	7.0	7.1
Teacher salaries	7.3	7.8	7.6
Hours of homework per week	7.2	7.3	6.3
Number of students	7.2	7.2	6.7
Percent of students who go on to a four-year college	7.0	6.9	6.8
Percent of students with an "A" or "B" average	7.0	6.5	5.8
Number of students per computer	6.9	6.4	6.1
Percent of parents who attend parent-teacher conferences	6.4	6.6	6.3
Demographics of students	4.5	4.6	5.0

From A Plus Communications, Arlington, Virginia

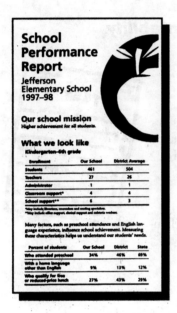

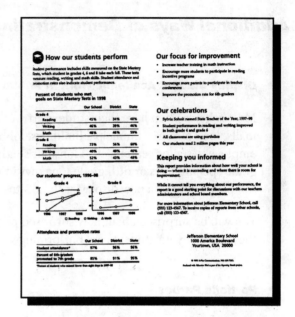

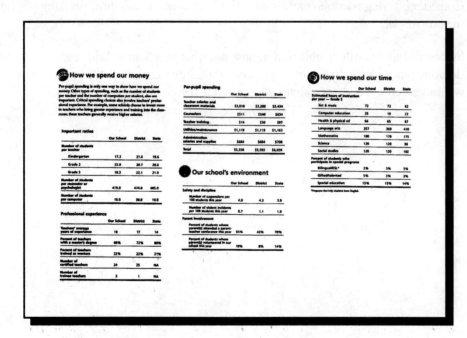

Additional Ways of Demonstrating Accountability

❖ *Display Student Academic Work in Public Settings*

Most schools often have their student art work posted at banks, malls, local airports, municipal buildings, lobbies of local major employers, senior centers, etc. Consider sending your third grade spelling tests or fifth grade long division and writing samples as part of a new display at these sites.

You will be surprised about how surprised people will be when they see that your students are performing so well.

❖ *Portfolio Parties*

Consider offering portfolio parties after the first, second, and third marking periods in your school.

Selected students will be able to demonstrate what they learned through demonstration. Keep the "party" to about 90 minutes and select those projects that will enlighten the audience about what is really happening in your school.

8 Ideas That Work

Practical Ways to Involve People

The most direct way to engage support for your school is to involve people. This section is full of ideas that you and others in your school can use to develop greater support from the many diverse publics that touch your school.

On the next few pages, you'll find practical ideas to help you deal with students, parents, teachers, non-teaching staff, business and community leaders, senior citizens, elected officials, and the news media. All these ideas have worked some place, are cost effective, and can be replicated easily.

Two words of caution:

❖ ***Don't try to do too many things at once.*** Implement activities as part of an overall plan. It's always best to do a good job with one or two new ideas first and then move on to others.

❖ While all of these ideas have worked in some school or community, ***you are the best judge of your needs, your resources, and your community.*** Having an overall plan will help ensure success.

Dealing with Students

❖ Learn the names of as many students as you can and greet them as they get off the bus, eat in the cafeteria, or walk through the hallways. Knowing students' names helps demonstrate your interest in them.

❖ Turn your business cards into happygrams. One elementary school principal writes a positive note on his business card whenever he sees a student do something positive and gives it to the youngster. The student feels good and usually takes it home to a parent.

❖ Assign a veteran student to each newcomer. Veterans can show new students to lockers and classes, eat lunch with them, introduce them to other students, and serve as positive role models.

❖ Find ways to recognize students — sending congratulatory letters, posting names on a bulletin board, or drawing attention to them at a recognition assembly or in announcements on the public address system. But be sure to honor all who deserve recognition— scholars, athletes, and those who perform community or school services.

❖ Create a peer tutoring program with a feeder school. Everyone benefits through such a program. The older students have a chance to serve and are recognized for it, while you strengthen the education program for the younger kids. Plus, it's a great way to market your school to prospective clients.

❖ Create a *Student of the Week* bulletin board or other area to recognize student achievements. You could display their photos, samples of their work, or newspaper articles about them.

❖ Take students to your civic club meeting and introduce them to the club. That practice can recognize a student who does something special, and also shows off some of your top youngsters to community leaders.

❖ Involve a student committee in planning school assemblies.

❖ Establish a partnership with local businesses to recognize student success. Businesses could provide discount coupons for students who improve their academic record or achieve a certain GPA.

❖ Have foreign exchange students from your school visit feeder schools to discuss their countries.

❖ Develop a Grade-a-Thon project where students can earn pledge money for a scholarship fund or new materials by obtaining A's and B's on their report card. Students can recruit pledges from parents, grandparents, or community members.

❖ Mail home congratulatory letters addressed to elementary school students. Kids this age love to get mail. It will make the recognition even better when parents ask what's in the envelope.

❖ Use photos of students in different aspects of school life — in classrooms, on the playground, in science lab — on your walls. It recognizes students and communicates what your school is all about.

❖ Establish a day when students can shadow the principal, school secretary, or custodian. This can reward students and also help build bridges between your staff and youngsters.

❖ Produce a short (10-minute) video on your school for prospective clients. You can show it at feeder schools, at events in your school for new students, and at parent meetings. You could also encourage people to check it out of the library to view it at home.

❖ Try to have at least one positive comment on every report card. If there is a positive note, student morale will be higher and parents will be more supportive.

Dealing with Parents

❖ With the hectic schedules many people have these days, some parents can't always attend a school performance to see their son or daughter. Consider videotaping school plays and other activities or assemblies and encouraging parents to check the video out of the library if they can't attend the event.

❖ Make sure you have a consistent vehicle that is the official record for school news — a parent newsletter published regularly would fulfill this function. It should include important dates, deadlines, and meeting notices, but it should also publicize student achievements and class activities.

❖ Establish an open-door policy or some other way for parents to obtain accurate answers to their questions about school. It's a wise use of time to clear up any misunderstanding before rumors start spreading throughout the community.

❖ Encourage teachers and other staff to communicate positive news about students to parents. Happygrams still work, as do notes and positive phone calls home. Invite parents of youngsters who will be attending your school next year to an evening meeting where they can learn about the

curriculum, policies, and activities. Encourage them to talk with current parents to get their perspective.

❖ Schedule some parent meetings when working parents can attend, including parent-teacher conferences and recognition events. This practice demonstrates that your school is customer friendly.

❖ Make sure important matters, such as policies, key dates, and ways to get questions answered, are publicized in the school handbook and that every parent receives a copy of the handbook.

❖ Develop a Welcome Wagon for new parents. This could be done by a student group, such as the National Honor Society chapter, or a parent group.

❖ Create a list of tips on parenting in your parents' newsletter or in a special parenting brochure. Better yet, run an evening class on parenting skills.

❖ Publish a calendar of key dates that parents need to know. The calendar could also include student photos or artwork.

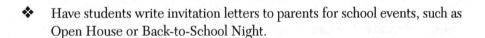

❖ Provide *I Have an Honor Roll Student at XXX School* bumper stickers. Plus distribute pup tent folders saying the same message that parents can place on their office desks.

❖ Have students write invitation letters to parents for school events, such as Open House or Back-to-School Night.

❖ Establish a recognition program for parents who contribute to the school or who work especially hard with their youngster. Publicize those individuals as role models for other parents.

Dealing with Teachers

❖ Urge parents to thank teachers and share positive comments — not just complain when problems arise.

❖ Give teachers quality professional development time to sharpen their skills. Something as simple as a period to read or time to visit surrounding schools can do wonders for morale.

❖ Have the principal teach a class for a teacher. Not only is that gesture appreciated by the teacher, it demonstrates that the principal cares about students. In fact, all members of the school's administrative team could teach an occasional class.

❖ Work with local businesses to establish summer internships for interested teachers. This can provide additional revenue for teachers and also help them remain current in their field.

❖ Send birthday cards to teachers and congratulate them on the staff lounge bulletin board.

❖ Recognize teachers and other staff in the school newsletter and staff bulletins for awards, new classroom initiatives, and other successes. Also praise them at PTA or advisory council meetings.

❖ Do whatever you can to make teachers feel as professional as possible. Good teachers work as hard as anyone else, but sometimes they don't even have convenient access to a telephone.

❖ Have a special place in your heart for substitute teachers — their job is tough. Consider these support items: Post a Polaroid photo of substitutes in the staff lounge so other teachers know who they are. Visit the classrooms of substitutes, especially early in the day. Show them you care about them. Send appreciation letters to subs who are outstanding.

❖ Develop partnerships with local businesses and community groups to recognize teachers, especially during Teacher Appreciation Week. Recognition might include certificates for dinner at a local restaurant, a congratulatory letter from the mayor, an invitation to a civic club's breakfast meeting, or discounts at local merchants.

Dealing with Non-Teaching Staff

❖ Be certain all staff get essential information about the school. Custodians are likely to talk about a new instructional program; bus drivers may spread their beliefs about the dress policy. Professional support staff delivers frequent, credible information. You must make sure that all staff have accurate information.

❖ Send birthday cards and recognize other personal celebrations.

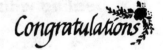

❖ Urge support staff to make suggestions and share ideas. Frankly, the school custodian might be the best person to recommend ways to make school maintenance more cost-effective. Value their opinions.

❖ Encourage support staff to assume new responsibilities. One school secretary writes a newsletter on student awards and classroom achievements; a custodian created a club for at-risk students where they work with him on school improvements.

❖ Recognize support staff publicly for their accomplishments at a PTA or staff meeting. Report their successes in the school newsletter and staff bulletin.

❖ Make sure that all staff feel comfortable using the staff lounge.

❖ Eat in the cafeteria. Show the food service staff you appreciate their work.

❖ Ride a school bus occasionally. Learn about the challenges bus drivers face, and show bus drivers you care about them and their concerns.

❖ Don't overlook support staff when it comes to professional development.

❖ Give support staff the opportunity to shine in front of the faculty. Encourage them to share a special interest like photography or scuba diving at a staff meeting. Sometimes this may lead to mini-lessons for students in classrooms.

Dealing with Business and Community Leaders

❖ Offer to have student groups perform for organizations throughout your community (such as Chamber of Commerce, Realty Board, Library Guild, and the like). This activity doesn't have to happen during the holiday season only.

❖ Host community leaders for a breakfast or lunch at your school. Have your students meet the community leaders and lead them on a tour of the school after the event so leaders can see what students learn in school today.

❖ Volunteer to speak about your school at civic and community group meetings.

❖ Give away leftover publications. Give yearbooks, school newspapers, or other publications that promote the success of your school to local doctor and dentist offices. People frequently read while waiting for their appointment.

❖ Publish brochures that describe the quality of your instructional program and your school's achievements. Give these to real estate agents, business leaders, employers… to anyone who may be attracting new people into your community.

Dealing with Senior Citizens

❖ Distribute Golden Passes that give senior citizens free admittance to school events — athletic contests, band concerts, and drama presentations.

❖ Encourage seniors to use school hallways before and after school for walking exercise.

❖ Encourage seniors to teach mini-lessons about a hobby, a trip, or local historic event that they may have experienced.

❖ Establish a pen-pal relationship between elementary school students and senior citizens. It shows the seniors that your students care, and it's also good education for your students.

❖ Arrange for various student groups to frequently visit senior centers.

❖ Establish service projects for students to conduct at senior centers (for instance, delivering Easter baskets, decorating during holidays, visiting seniors on Grandparents Day).

Dealing with Elected Officials

❖ Invite an elected official to teach a government or other class.

❖ Offer artwork from students to elected officials for display in government offices.

❖ Volunteer to serve as an elected official's resource on educational issues. Elected officials could be looking for interpretation and advice when a school issue arises.

❖ Invite elected officials to attend student events, such as plays and concerts. Let them see first-hand the results of the programs they fund. Better yet, have one of the students invite them.

❖ Develop a list of your school's achievements and send it to elected officials.

❖ Put elected officials on the mailing list for school publications.

❖ Remember to thank elected leaders for their support of your schools.

General Advice

❖ Consider which messages you want people to receive from your school. Brainstorm ideas with staff and key advisers. Announce these messages to staff and print them on tent cards placed by every telephone. Whenever someone answers the phone, the card will remind them to deliver that key message.

❖ Start See-for-Yourself Days. Students at schools in Adams County (CO) receive three invitations to give to anyone in the community. The invitation urges people to come to the school to see how learning has changed from the "good old days."

❖ Decorate hallways, bulletin boards, offices, and other spots with student art and writing to demonstrate their talent.

❖ Develop a school theme that delivers a message that represents your school — *Sunnyside Elementary Puts Students First*. Use your theme everywhere — on letterheads, envelopes, newsletters, and school's outdoor message board.

❖ Use the school message board to deliver success messages (For instance, 6th Grade Club Cleans Creek Bed). Too many schools use this board merely to announce sports games, and leave that message up two months after the game has been played.

❖ Put a suggestion box in a prominent place and encourage students, parents, staff, and visitors to use it.

❖ Print postcards asking people for their opinions, questions, or suggestions about your school; include your school address and postage. It's a great way to get feedback. Put the cards in well-traveled areas in your community.

❖ Invite district office personnel into your school for an exciting instructional activity, competition, or performance. Show off your students and teachers.

❖ Send short items of community interest to the various publications that serve your community (for instance, religious bulletins, civic club newsletters, local business newsletters, etc.).

❖ Encourage student leaders and staff to walk through the neighborhood closest to your school. Let your neighbors see who you are and that you care.

❖ Welcome visitors at your school. Greet them promptly in the office, smile and make the visitor sign more customer-friendly. Instead of *Warning—all visitors must report to the office*; try *Welcome to Our School—please register at the office*.

A Fun Way to Collect "What's Right" Data

A great way to start this process of promoting your school is to schedule a 90-minute brainstorming session for the entire school staff — teachers, aides, secretaries, custodians, administrators, counselors, psychologists... *everyone*.

The purpose of this session is to simply answer the question, **"What's right with my school?"** This will be a fun meeting and will help develop a feeling of pride among staff members as they see all the accomplishments of your school.

How to Conduct a Brainstorming Session

Here are key steps to conducting this brainstorming activity:

❶ **Invite all staff members.** Consider including some key parents and volunteers as well.

❷ **Seat everyone at round tables with no more than eight at each table.** Get a mix of individuals at each table — you don't want the entire science department or fifth grade team at the same table. You may need to assign tables or have the participants draw a table number as they enter the room.

❸ **Briefly explain the rules of brainstorming,** remembering that some participants may not have done this before.

❹ **Have each table select a leader and recorder.**

❺ **Introduce the task.** Explain the need to focus attention on your school's accomplishments and getting that information to the community. Indicate that this activity will help to develop community support for your school and those working in it. Challenge participants to give their best to this session since the results will be the foundation for this confidence-building project.

What to Focus on

Pay attention to at least five areas:

❖ Student successes, such as scholarships and awards;

❖ Staff honors, such as Teacher-of-the-Year awards or articles featuring a staff member in a professional journal or newspaper;

❖ Student contributions, such as the science club's cleaning up a creek bed in your community;

❖ Graduates — those who attended your school and are now respected adults; and

❖ Special programs and activities that make your school different from others.

What to Do

❖ Have each table spend 10 minutes on each item. Make each group list as many accomplishments as possible.

❖ Then have the table leaders report their lists to the entire group.

❖ You could award a prize to the table with the greatest number of accomplishments.

❖ Be sure that someone writes down all the responses so that you can use them later.

❖ Once the brainstorming is completed, compile the best ideas that can be used in your school's "What's Right" campaign.

❖ Distribute this final list to all staff — it's their ammunition to respond to questions about your school. Some schools or districts print such lists on cards that can fit into a shirt pocket or purse; others spread the news out over the year by featuring a few items in each newsletter.

❖ Most parents want to brag about their child's school. This process gives you the ammunition to do just that!

Outdoor Message Boards and Marquees

Private industry spends millions each year on outdoor advertising. Too often schools ignore this medium or use it only to carry dates of events. Some principals use the outdoor marquee to give their school a personality·so it stands out from the crowd.

Gather some of your more creative staff members or use your entire staff to brainstorm items to put on your outdoor marquee. Here's one to consider:

NSPRA Elementary School

Advice to Kindergarten Parents:

Read to your child every day. By the third grade, we will know who followed this advice and who didn't.

Source: Unidentified suburban Boston Principal
in *The Washington Post*

Use Those Business Cards Creatively

If you are like most principals, you probably wonder what you will do with all those business cards sitting back in your office drawer. Kay Woefel, a principal in Illinois, uses her cards in the following ways:

❖ She writes "catch 'em being good" messages on the back of her cards and you can be sure those business cards reach home that afternoon.

❖ She stashes some cards in school library books with the message, "Will the finder of this card please join the principal for sustained silent reading tomorrow." After they both read together, another card is sent home saying all the right things about the student and reading.

❖ She also hands out her cards to everyone at a newcomer teas, kindergarten registration, and reminds participants that "no question is too small."

When Rewards Are Called for... Instant Positive Communication

Some principals and teachers with either a cordless or cellular phone now make it a practice to either call a parent at home or at work when a student does something "calling" for recognition. Frequently, the student is asked to call his or her mom or dad, and tell them that the principal wants to talk with them.

You can imagine the surprise when the principals reports, "What a great kid you have, because today...!"

Making the call in the middle of a class is often a major motivator for other students as well. How often have you gotten a positive phone call about your child in the middle of the day? It turns into a memorable moment that can be replicated at least once a week.

9 Additional Resources

Resources

In this section, you'll find these additional resources:

❖ *Resources for Community Engagement available from the National Association of Elementary School Principals*

❖ *Resources for Community Engagement available from the National School Public Relations Association*

❖ *Getting Started with Cable in the Classroom*

❖ *Resource Materials for The Child Development Project*

Principals in the Public

Resources for Community Engagement
available from the
National Association of Elementary School Principals

- **Positive Discipline in the Classroom**
  Learn Methods of Working Together to Solve Student Problems

- **Ways We Want Our Class To Be**
  A Hands on Approach for schools which can be used to implement classroom
  meetings by addressing academic and social issues

- **Bully Free Classroom**
  More than 100 prevention and intervention strategies you can start using immediately

- **Yardsticks: Children in the Classroom Ages 4-14**
  An easy to use reference to expectations about children's growth and development in
  the classroom

- **Parents On Your Side**
  Turn parents into partners with this step-by-step involvement program

- **Involving Parents in Schools**
  Involve parents and gain community support

- **The Little Things Make a Big Difference - Video**
  Planning an effective parent education workshop

- **Little Beginnings - Video**
  Help prepare children for school

- **The Little Things Make a Big Difference – Parent Booklet**
  Creative Parent Education

- **Little Beginnings – Parent Booklet**
  Offers reassuring advice for new parents

- **The Apple of Your Eye**
  Now grandparents can help grandchildren succeed in school

- **School, Family and Community Partnership**
  A design program focuses on student learning and school success

- **Vital Information for Quality Schools**
  Practical ideas and research that helps provide dynamic leadership for schools, staff, students and the community

  - **An award-winning web site hosting a web of opportunities and visibility for our members by offering resources materials, strategies for success and School, Family and Community Partnerships**

To order or obtain additional information about these resources visit our shopping mall and On-line catalog at: www.naesp.org or contact:

National Association of Elementary School Principals
1615 Duke Street
Alexandria, Virginia 22314-3483
Phone: (800) 386-2377 – (703) 684-3345
FAX: (800) 396-2377

www.naesp.org

Resources for Community Engagement
available from the
National School Public Relations Association

- **School Public Relations: Building Confidence in Education**
  A comprehensive book on school public relations and what it can do for your schools and communities.

- **School-Based Management: A Communication Workshop Kit**
  A step-by-step guide for building commitment, improving communication, and increasing involvement.

- **It Starts on the Frontline**
  A communication newsletter for principals full of practical ideas including resources, fillers for newsletters and reproducible tip sheets.

- **Making and Marketing Your School the School of Choice**
  A practical handbook for marketing your school, building support and enhancing your reputation.

- **Multilingual Welcome Poster**
  This ready-to-hang, full-color poster warmly welcomes visitors in 25 languages.

- **See For Yourself!: A Campaign to Build Support for Your Schools**
  A booklet of ideas and tools for starting a campaign to build support and understanding for your school.

- **Parent Guides**
  Inexpensive booklets on three topics to help parents help their children and feel comfortable at school.

- **Thinking About the Unthinkable: Seeking Solutions to School Violence**
  A video overview of strategies and guidelines for dealing with a crisis and the aftermath. Includes a reproducible discussion guide to engage stakeholders in addressing the issue of violence in schools.

- **Public Engagement — "A Quiet Revolution"**
  An NSPRA Bonus Item of tips and resources for starting a public engagement process.

- **NSPRA National Seminar**
  Each July, NSPRA offers a three-day seminar for school leaders on all facets of building trust and support for schools. The NSPRA Seminar is known for its practical, hands-on sessions, ability to stimulate creative ideas, and the friendliness of colleagues helping colleagues.

- **WWW.NSPRA.ORG**
  An award-winning web site offering a host of valuable information and resources on communication, community engagement and public relations.

To order or obtain additional information about these resources see our On-line Catalog at **www.nspra.org** *or contact:*

National School Public Relations Association
15948 Derwood Rd.
Rockville, MD 20855
Phone: (301) 519-0496   FAX: (301) 519-0494

Getting Started with CABLE IN THE CLASSROOM

It's easy to bring Cable in the Classroom's motivating, commercial-free resources into your classroom.
Just follow these steps:

Start with your curriculum. Wish your students could see, as well as read about, how a bill becomes law? Looking for real-world demonstrations of mathematics concepts? Trying to find ways to draw reluctant students into class discussions and writing projects? Cable in the Classroom programs can help. And since these programs are copyright-cleared for at least a year, you decide when and how to use them.

Call your local cable company to request a free cable connection, if your school doesn't already have one. Member cable companies provide this service to accredited public and private K-12 schools passed by cable in their communities. Some local cable companies offer training for school staff, complimentary copies of *Cable in the Classroom* magazine and the latest information on new Cable in the Classroom initiatives.

Review the schedule of upcoming educational programs printed in *Cable in the Classroom* magazine each month or search our database at www.ciconline.org to find appropriate programs for the subjects and grade levels you teach throughout the school year.

Look to *Cable in the Classroom* magazine for information about free or low-cost curriculum support materials—teaching suggestions, student activities, project ideas—created by Cable in the Classroom members to accompany their educational programs. Link to our members from the Cable in the Classroom Web site for additional resources, such as downloadable lesson plans and links to related sites.

Program your school's VCR (or recruit community volunteers to tape at home) and tape the selected programs. Most Cable in the Classroom programs air in the early morning hours while you sleep, making it easy for busy teachers, media specialists, and volunteers to capture the resources schools need.

Catalogue your videos and accompanying resource materials according to the concepts, topics, and skills you teach, making specific tapes easier to find as you plan your lessons. Note the recording and the erasing dates to help you stay within copyright guidelines.

Preview each recorded program to make sure it fits your needs. What parts of the program are relevant to your curriculum? At what point in your plans will the video be most useful? How can the video be used to support students with special needs?

View the tape with your students to demonstrate a skill, illustrate an idea, reinforce a concept, and promote discussion. Show only the most appropriate parts of the tape. You needn't show an hour-long documentary, if only one or two short segments really fit your lesson plans. Stop the tape occasionally to explain and emphasize key points and check student comprehension.
You're on your way to building a free library of curriculum-based, commercial-free resources!

1800 N. Beauregard Street, Suite 100, Alexandria, VA 22311 (Tel.) 703-845-1400 (Fax) 703-845-1409
ON THE INTERNET: www.ciconline.org EMAIL: cic@ciconline.org EDUCATOR HOTLINE: 800-743-5355
Design and illustration by Eric S. MacDicken ©Cable in the Classroom 2000

The Child Development Project

The Child Development Project (CDP) is a research-based school improvement initiative from the Developmental Studies Center (phone: 800-666-7270, Oakland, CA). Successful implementation has been demonstrated to support elementary schools as "caring communities of learners" and provide protection against the risk of substance abuse. Visit the DSC website at www.devstu.org or see detailed CDP information at www.samhsa.gov/csap/modelprograms

Phase One

At Home in Our Schools

The 136-page book focuses on schoolwide activities that help educators and parents create caring school communities. It includes ideas about leadership, step-by-step guidelines for 15 activities, and reproducible planning resources and suggestions for teachers. The 12-minute overview video is designed for staff meetings and parent gatherings. The 48-page study guide structures a series of organizing meetings for teachers, parents, and administrators.

Book: *$14.95/136 pages/ISBN: 1-885603-00-2/Item # CBC001*

The At Home in Our Schools Collegial Study Package *includes the book, the overview video, and the study guide. $47.50/Item # CBP000*

That's My Buddy! Friendship and Learning across the Grades

This book is a practical guide for two buddy teachers or a whole staff. It draws on the experiences of teachers from DSC's Child Development Project schools across the country. The 12-minute overview video is designed for use at staff meetings and the 48-page study guide structures a series of teacher meetings for collegial study and support once a buddies program is launched.

Book: *$14.95/144 pages/ISBN: 1-885603-81-9/Item # BBB001*

The Buddies Collegial Study Package *includes the book, the overview video, and the study guide. $47.50/Item # BBP000*

Homeside Activities (K–6)

Seven separate collections of activities by grade level help teachers, parents, and children communicate. Each 128-page collection has an introductory overview, 18 reproducible take-home activities in both English and Spanish, and suggestions for integrating the activities into the classroom. The 12-minute English overview video is designed for parent gatherings and can also be used in staff development. A separate Spanish overview video is specifically designed for parent meetings. The 48-page study guide structures a series of teacher meetings for collegial study.

Each book: *$13.95/128 pages/Please specify grade level desired.*

Set of six books (Grades K–5): *$75.00/Item # HABS00*

Homeside Activities Overview Video (English, one for all grades): *$29.95/12 minutes/ISBN: 1-885603-79-7 Item # HAV001*

Actividades Familiares Overview Video (Spanish, one for all grades): *Unique footage portraying two bilingual classrooms and seven family settings; not a translation of English overview. $29.95/12 minutes / ISBN: 1-57621-148-7/Item # SHAV01*

The Homeside Activities Collegial Study Package *includes 6 books (one each grades K–5), the overview video, the study guide, and a 31-minute video visiting 3 classrooms and parents working at home with their children. $150.00/Item # HAP000*

Ways We Want Our Class to Be: Class Meetings That Build Commitment to Kindness and Learning

The 120-page book describes how to use class meetings to build a caring classroom community and address the academic and social issues that arise in an elementary school classroom. In addition to tips on getting started, setting ground rules, and facilitating the meetings, 14 guidelines for specific class meetings are included. The 20-minute overview video introduces 3 kinds of class meetings. The 48-page study guide helps structure a series of teacher meetings for collegial study. In-depth video documentation shows 7 classrooms where students are involved in planning and decision making, checking in on learning and behavior, and problem solving.

Book: *$14.95/120 pages/ISBN: 1-885603-80-0/Item # CMB001*

The Ways We Want Our Class to Be Collegial Study Package *includes the book, the overview video, the study guide, and 99 minutes of video documenting 7 classrooms. $199.00/Item # CMP000*

Among Friends: Classrooms Where Caring and Learning Prevail

In classroom vignettes and conversations with teachers, this book provides concrete ideas for building caring learning communities in elementary school classrooms. CDP Program Director Marilyn Watson and educator Joan Dalton take us into classrooms where teachers demonstrate how they promote children's intellectual, social, and ethical development. A chapter on theory and research provides a coherent rationale for the approach.

Book: *$16.95/208 pages/ISBN: 1-57621-142-8/Item # AMF001*

The Among Friends Package *includes the book, 4 video cassettes visiting 8 classrooms (106 minutes), the Collegial Study Guide, the Teacher Educator Guide, and a packet of 20 teacher reflection guides. $230.00/Item # AMP000*

To order or obtain further information about CDP or these resources, please contact us:

Developmental Studies Center

2000 Embarcadero, Suite 305 • Oakland, CA 94606-5300
E-mail: pubs@devstu.org

USA Phone: (800) 666-7270 or (510) 533-0213 • Fax: (510) 464-3670

Blueprints for a Collaborative Classroom

Demonstrating how to integrate collaboration throughout the curriculum, this 192-page "how-to" collection of partner and small-group activities is organized into 25 categories that range from quick partner interviews to complex research projects. Over 250 activity suggestions are included for all elementary grades. In addition, "Fly on the Wall" vignettes offer insights from real classrooms.

Book: $16.95/192 pages/ISBN: 1-57621-141-X/Item # BCC000

The Blueprints for a Collaborative Classroom Package includes the book, an overview video, 3 video cassettes visiting 6 classrooms (85 min.), the Collegial Study Guide, the Teacher Educator Guide, and a packet of 20 teacher reflection guides. $199.00/Item # BLP000

Reading, Thinking & Caring: Literature-Based Reading (Grades K–3)

A children's literature program to help students love to read, think deeply and critically, and care about how they treat themselves and others. Individual teaching guides have been developed for over 100 classic, contemporary, and multicultural titles (fiction and non-fiction) for reading aloud and partner reading. Each 3- to 10-day guide helps teachers build reading comprehension and social/emotional literacy. A take-home activity in English and Spanish is included to involve parents in their children's life at school. Each guide sold separately or in grade-level sets; accompanying trade books also available.

Each teacher guide: $13.95/16 to 48 pages (varies).

Complete grade level sets include Teacher Guides, Program Manual, and Bibliography in binder, along with trade books. $450 to $550 (approx. 25 to 30 titles per grade level; varies). PLEASE REQUEST CURRENT CATALOG FOR FURTHER DETAILS AND COMPLETE LIST OF TITLES BY GRADE LEVEL.

Reading for Real: Literature-Based Reading (Grades 4–8)

A literature-based program to engage the student's conscience while building comprehension and providing important reading, writing, speaking, and listening experiences. Teaching guides are available for over 125 classic, contemporary, and multicultural titles (fiction, non-fiction narrative, and expository). Some are designed to be read aloud by the teacher and some to be read together by student partners. Each 1- to 3-week guide includes a take-home activity (in English) to involve parents. Each guide sold separately or in grade-level sets; accompanying trade books also available.

Each teacher guide: $13.95/16 to 48 pages (varies).

Complete grade level sets include Teacher Guides, Program Manual, and Bibliography in binder, along with trade books and overview video. $450 to $500 (approx. 25 titles per grade level; varies). PLEASE REQUEST CURRENT CATALOG FOR FURTHER DETAILS AND COMPLETE LIST OF TITLES BY GRADE LEVEL.

Number Power (Grades K–6)

Each of nine teacher resource books offers 3 replacement units (8–12 lessons per unit) that foster students' mathematical and social development. Students collaboratively investigate problems, develop their number sense, enhance their mathematical reasoning and communication skills, and learn to work together effectively. (Grades K, 1, 4, 5, and 6 have one volume each; grades 2 and 3 have two volumes each.)

A complete supplemental program (including blackline masters), Number Power meets NCTM Standards and is recommended by the U.S. Dept. of Education.

Each book: $19.95/approx. 200 pages/ISBN: 0-201-varies/Please indicate grade level desired.

Phase Two

Prices are subject to change without notice. The above prices are current as of March, 2000.

For shipping and handling:

Orders under $30 — add $4.50
Orders from $30–$100 — add $6.00
Orders over $100 — add 6%
Orders outside U.S. — varies; please inquire